Mixed Ability Classes

Luke Prodromou

MACMILLAN
PUBLISHERS

First published 1992
Reprinted 1994

Published by
MACMILLAN PUBLISHERS LTD
London and Basingstoke

ISBN 0 – 333 – 49386 – 9

Printed in Malaysia

A catalogue record for this book is available from the British Library.

In memory of my mother, Antigone

Acknowledgements

I would like to thank all those teachers of large, mixed ability classes in Greece and other countries who have taken part over the years in seminars on the subject, and who have given me so much to think about concerning the myth of the 'poor' language learner. I would also like to thank Mario Rinvolucri and John Morgan for their inspiration; Andrew Wilcox for his jokes; my editor Catherine Gray for her tolerance and understanding; and, finally, my mixed ability family for their patience during the writing and rewriting of this book.

Contents

CHAPTER 1 | Introduction

The myth of the 'bad' language learner

> **Task:** The following terms are frequently used to refer to certain kinds of students. Which would you say are positive and which negative in meaning?
>
> weak   low achiever   bad   reluctant
> poor   problem   slow   remedial
> difficult   less able   less competent   bottom

This book is about those learners for whom we have mostly negative names. The words we use about people and things often determine the way we see them, and, more significantly in the learning context, the way we talk *about* learners affects the way we talk *to* them. Thus, students of English as a foreign language can be educated into failure, just as children are often educated into a low opinion of themselves by the words their parents use or their tone of voice.

It is difficult even to talk about the mixed ability class without seeming to subscribe to a kind of fatalism about the abilities of the less confident, outspoken or high-achieving. They are condemned to failure simply because there seems no way of talking about them which does not suggest deficiency of some kind. We constantly slip into the habit of thinking about them in terms of their weaknesses rather than their strengths.

The origins of this book go back further than my involvement in language teaching, going beyond the EFL classroom to other learning situations. The following are three stories which should illustrate my point.

Tubby and Titch the twins

Tubby and Titch were twins. They were mixed ability twins: Tubby learned easily and quickly, Titch found learning new things slow and painful. Titch wouldn't eat anything new until months had passed; he wouldn't join in at a party until it was nearly over; he was afraid of learning to ride his new bicycle in case he fell off.

But at least in all these instances, he would get there in the end. The fact that he fell off his bicycle shows that he was riding it in the first place, and after all, falling off can be a necessary prelude to learning to balance.

11-plus or minus?

I remember teachers who, faced with classes of pupils who had failed their 11-plus, had obviously decided that their young charges were only fit for factory fodder. And that is how most of them ended up. Other, more enlightened teachers taught their pupils to believe in themselves and their potential for growth.

K.M. was a pupil in a secondary modern school. He came bottom of the class in most subjects. He only excelled in the number of canings and detentions he got; he was the leader of a playground gang known as The Three Musketeers. When he was in the fifth form, his headmaster called him to his office. K.M.'s fingers tingled with the expectation of another caning as he walked into the all-too familiar room. The headmaster told him to sit down, which was odd, and informed him that he had been appointed Head Prefect of the school, which was even odder still.

A year later, encouraged by the same headmaster who had punished him so many times, K.M. left his secondary modern school to go to a grammar school where he could take university entrance exams. There, he discovered he needed French to get into university. He had never studied it before; in his old school, they had done woodwork and metalwork instead. The French teacher told him that it was too late to try and get an 'O' level in one year. But K.M. said he could do it. And he did.

Eventually, he found himself at university. He studied for an MA and became a university lecturer.

The kitchen: sink or swim?

H.D. left school in the fourth year having been told she was wasting both her time and the school's. She got married and worked in a shop and had babies. She studied the kitchen walls for hours and weeks, months and years. She reached the point where she could have drawn the kitchen in the minutest detail with her eyes closed. This went on until she couldn't have any more children and the little ones had become big ones and no longer needed her. At last, at the age of 35, she went to university to study sociology.

This book has gained much impetus from those women who, denied a place in higher education when they finished school, came back fighting later in life, sweated perhaps over Open University course-books, and went on to get a degree as 'mature students'. There is a kind of defeatism amongst women in many parts of the world as regards education, which is similar to the kind of fatalism encountered amongst so-called 'poor' language learners.

> **Task:** Write a brief account of a story from your own experience which illustrates the way learners have overcome the low expectations that teachers or parents have had of them.

There are undoubtedly many more stories like these to be shared, stories that throw light on the way schools and families categorise 'good' and 'bad', and on the way some teachers help students to grow and others impede that growth. This book assumes that the 'bad' learner is a myth, born on the one hand from the belief that some students either simply do not want to learn or are incapable of it and, on the other, from a narrow view of what teaching involves. It is my assumption in this book that

- students *do* want to learn;
- learning can be a pleasurable experience;
- no-one likes to fail;
- weakness is simply the tip of an iceberg of strength;
- teaching English as a foreign language is an *educational* practice.

It would be short-sighted not to acknowledge how entrenched the belief in innate failure can be, and not to recognise that this belief is based on the concrete experience of teachers, and parents, all over the world. Unquestioned beliefs may blind us, however, to possibilities and alternative explanations. There is a danger that the attitude expressed by 'They just don't want to learn' may become engrained, and frustrate the potential of students and other learners whose situations are rather more complex. Such statements close windows and slam doors.

> **Task:** Here are some more things teachers of English have said about the mixed ability class. The teachers who expressed these views were non-native speakers of English. I have divided their views into problems, suggestions and questions.
>
> 1 Which of the problems do you share?
> 2 Can you add your own suggestions to the list?
> 3 How would you answer the questions put by teachers of mixed ability groups?
>
> *1 Problems*
>
> 'Some of the students are advanced and lose interest in the class, and some of them hardly know any English at all and are forced to quit.'
>
> 'There are some students who always participate in the classroom, and others who seem totally indifferent.'
>
> 'Bad students are indifferent.'
>
> 'Some of them are aggressive, and a domineering teacher can create an inferiority complex in weak students.'

'The problem is that most students can't communicate in English. They can't understand the teacher when she speaks and, as a matter of fact, can't answer questions.'

'The teacher finds it difficult to teach the same kind of material to all the students.'

'Teachers are the main cause of the problem, by expecting students to learn the same things at the same time.'

'They get separated into different factions and l can't hold them together.'

'Weak students feel disappointed and don't want to take part in the lesson.'

2 Suggestions

'You have to explain again and again in a different way – or in their native language, if you realise that it will take up too much time otherwise.'

'Give different groups different tasks.'

'I suggest that different levels of ability should be separated either into different classes or different groups.'

'The thing I do is to ask more advanced students to be tolerant when they hear things they already know, and to help me make the beginners understand.'

'The First Certificate level students help their classmates in group-work or pair-work.'

'One needs to have special talent to be able to grade the tasks and to provide the right stimuli. (I'm afraid I don't always make the right choice.)'

3 Questions

'At the end of each year, should all pupils in a mixed ability class be examined on the same subjects at the same level?'

Your answer: _____

'Do you agree with the suggestion of dividing the class into levels?'

Your answer: _____

'Do you agree that sometimes what is important is just to communicate with the ones that are not going to learn English anyway? In that case, discussing problems in their native language is perhaps the only thing you can do.'

Your answer: _____

Approaches

Before going on to outline the approach taken in this book, I'd like to present the views of other writers on the subject.

● Group-work

Like the teachers quoted above, most writers who tackle the problem of mixed ability classes suggest that group-work is invaluable as a technique.

> 'Group-work is an obvious choice for mixed ability classes. A maximum number of students are active and occupied.'*(Scheibl, 1984)*

Although group-work is flexible enough to allow different students to work on different tasks according to their individual abilities, the danger is that the class will break up 'into different factions', as one of the teachers quoted above found. Patty Hemingway stresses the role the mother tongue has in this respect:

> 'Any strategy that enables the whole class to work together is useful . . . The use of the mother tongue may be an advantage, not a distraction, if it involves all students in the lesson, avoids frustrating misunderstandings, and encourages collaboration.'   *(Hemingway, 1986)*

● Remedial work

There are various ways of helping slower learners to consolidate old material while still sustaining the interest of the entire class. One of these is to recycle material by practising different aspects of it, using, for example, a grammatical structure in different contexts; the same text first for listening, then later for reading comprehension, or first as a dictation and then as a cloze test; or reworking dull textbook dialogues as drama activities. Another solution is to give students extra work to do at home, either written especially for the purpose or extracted from available textbooks. As Scheibl suggests,

> 'You could make cassette tapes available for home use, perhaps with key-words and key-points, so they can go over the lesson at their own pace at home.'   *(Scheibl, 1984)*

● One text, many levels

Pictures are an obvious example of material which is of indeterminate difficulty and can be used by students at different levels. However, conventional techniques such as dictation and cloze testing can also be made sensitive to the needs of the mixed ability class by simple adaptation. Rinvolucri (1986), for example, suggests giving out two versions of the same dictation: in one, half the words are left out, and in the other, about a fifth are missing. High-achieving students will write the dictation with no support, so in fact three different groups can work on the same task at levels which reflect their ability. The beauty of this technique is that once the teacher has finished dictating, the different groups will need to confer with each other to check their work.

A similar approach is possible with cloze texts: false beginners can be given a text in which every fourth word is missing, and real beginners one with every eighth word missing. (See also chapter 6 of this book for further ideas on this approach.)

● **Self-access**

If the circumstances permit, encouraging independent study through the use of self-access activities is an ideal approach to the mixed ability class. Self-access tasks and exercises allow students to work on material of their own choice and to monitor and check their own progress. As testing is a particularly thorny problem in mixed ability groups, self-access techniques are helpful in developing students' self-evaluation procedures. By checking their own work, they not only avoid the embarrassment of public assessment, but develop greater confidence in themselves.

● **The early finisher**

Many teachers will already have developed ways of dealing with early finishers, who quickly become restless and end up making mischief. (That's when the paper aeroplanes start to fly!) Hemingway (1986) suggests ways of keeping early finishers busy which include project work, the use of simplified readers, and writing further questions for the rest of the class.

Task: The following questionnaire summarises some of the solutions to the problems of the mixed ability class. How many of the techniques do you already use?

Do you . . .?

1 encourage co-operation and respect amongst your students?
2 accept all their contributions as valid and valuable?
3 use the mother tongue as an aid to learning?
4 use visuals that are open to interpretation at various levels?
5 involve the whole class in the checking phase?
6 use students' non-linguistic skills (for example, their knowledge of other subjects or their ability to draw or mimic)?
7 grade your worksheets, making them usable by students at different levels?
8 grade dictation and cloze exercises?
9 use drama techniques?
10 make the most of group-work?
11 practise learner training to help your students become more independent?
12 give your students a real choice when making decisions?
13 use information-gap techniques?
14 build checking and feedback into the exercises you set?
15 develop self-evaluation in your learners?
16 treat your students as people with a past and a future?
17 treat your students as people who think?
18 treat your students as people who feel?
19 encourage reading for pleasure?
20 have a store of supplementary tricks, such as games, jokes, puzzles, stories, etc. to deal with early finishers?

Analysis

All classes are, of course, mixed ability:

> 'We do not teach a group, but thirty separate people. Because of this, the problem of mixed abilities in the same room seems absolutely natural, and it is the idea of teaching a unitary lesson that seems odd.'
>
> *(Rinvolucri, 1986)*

Although there are mild and acute cases of mixed ability, all classes are made up of individuals who differ in any number of ways. The simplest way of looking at the class is in terms of language ability. It is obviously too reductive just to state that some students know a lot of English, and other know less, but distinctions can be made between specified levels of linguistic ability and between different skills: between phonology, structure and vocabulary, for example, or between discourse and communication. The successful language learner may well be adept at all these skills, but it does not necessarily follow that the weak learner rates equally poorly in them all. Learners usually have a variable rather than a uniform linguistic competence. If we are to build on the potential strengths of even the most apparently hopeless cases, then the knowledge that a student may be very weak at grammar, but less so at learning vocabulary may prove an important insight, and a first step towards helping their progression and development. Building on what the students already know has always been a good first premise.

But there is more to the learner than just language. Every learner brings into the classroom a whole complex of personal characteristics which influence their approach to what is happening there. They carry with them a world of experience and knowledge, feeling and ideology, which may help, or hinder, the acquisition of a foreign language. It seems that the best way to create an antipathy to learning is to treat the learner as empty-headed. The learner tends to react in self-defence, and discipline problems often follow. It is an important principle to see your students as *whole people* rather than as fragments of language (and this idea is pursued in chapters 5 and 8 of this book). The diagram below represents a more rounded view of the learner:

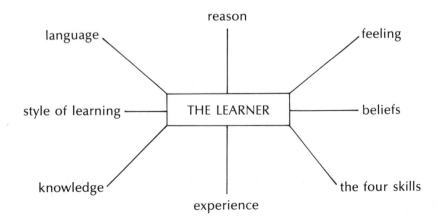

●Reason

Reason is important when dealing with grammar as a system and when engaging in any kind of problem-solving activity. In their attempt to maintain attention and discipline in a large mixed ability class, teachers often spoonfeed students with grammar rules, answers and definitions. Wherever possible, however, approaches should encourage students to discover rules for themselves through problem-solving activities, as this will ensure that their concentration is engaged and that their understanding is thorough and lasting.

●Feeling

The learners' feelings may raise or lower the barriers to language acquisition. In a sense, this whole book is about how to channel the learner's feelings towards acquiring language in a positive, pleasurable way. Chapters 9 and 10 in particular focus on the 'pleasure principle' in language learning, and motivating drama techniques (see chapter 8) are impossible without the learners' emotional commitment.

●Beliefs

A learner's beliefs form part of the cultural context in which all educational activity is carried out, and they are always relevant, whether directly or indirectly, implicitly or explicitly, when people communicate. Teachers also convey certain beliefs, about society and the role of the individual within it. They do this whenever they assert their authority over an undisciplined class, whenever they give or mark a test, whenever they rearrange their students in groups to work in collaboration or in competition with each other. It is as well to be aware of these, often unintended, 'ideological messages' and to channel them towards a greater trust between learner and teacher and, therefore, towards a more conducive language learning environment (see chapters 3 and 5).

●The four skills

Just as some learners may be good at vocabulary but weak at grammar, so others are good at listening but bad at speaking. Some have a knack for remembering new words or putting on an English accent, while others just like a quiet read. Consequently, a teaching style that sees the traditional four skills as an integrated whole will be more likely to meet the needs of a wide variety of learners than one which sees the skills as separate or as scaled according to importance. A teacher should know his or her students well enough to focus on the skills they need most, but at the same time should ensure that insecure students are given an opportunity to demonstrate and practise the skills they are most comfortable with. The emphasis on integrated skills and information-transfer techniques that accompanies the communicative approach to language learning has proved a positive development in the context of the mixed ability class (see chapters 6 and 7).

●Experience

Asking students to talk or write about things they have never had direct, or even indirect, experience of is a recipe for disaster in a mixed ability language class. The silence of so-called 'weak' learners may have little to do with their competence in the language, and rather more to do with their being confronted with questions that assume an experience of the world they do not have:

> 'We have the strange paradox that in mother-tongue teaching we emphasise the clarity of the child's ability to express himself, while in the foreign language we demand that he express a culture of which he has scarcely any experience.'   *(Brumfit, 1980)*

In giving learners the power of speech in a foreign language, it will be important to take into account not only their individual experience, but the culture of the society in which they live. This book takes a cross-cultural approach to the mixed ability class, recommending subject matter drawn from the students' own lives, as well as from Anglo-American and international cultures. Language learning cannot proceed if the students have nothing to say, especially about the world around them. Learning a foreign language should therefore be seen as part of the broader educational goal of learning to live in the modern world in an international – and global – sense (see chapter 5).

● Knowledge

Students may be top of the class in geography or physics, but not be very good at English. It is sometimes difficult to motivate students to take English seriously, particularly in societies where English has low status as a school subject. There are a number of approaches to this problem, but one that is frequently recommended is to make English the medium of instruction in other subjects. If English is used to discuss pop music, computers or sport, an apparently unmotivated student may suddenly come to life. Students should wherever possible be wearing their knowledge, not their ignorance, on their sleeve, and quizzes, project work and other activities can encourage this in the language classroom.

One vital area of knowledge the students possess is their own native language, and the careful use of this reservoir of knowledge in the mixed ability class will often open a way into the lesson for the weak learner (see chapter 5).

● Style of learning

Related to both experience and knowledge is the question of individual approaches to learning. These may be related to personality (whether, for instance, the student is introverted or extroverted) or to previous learning experience. Many students come from a rote-learning back-ground, but some have been exposed to group-work by their previous teacher; students may thus either expect the teacher to know and reveal everything, or be keen to discover things for themselves. All one can predict for certain about a class is that it will cover a wide variety of learning styles, and the teacher will have to be a highly skilful classroom manager to satisfy them all. Traditional lock-step teaching (whereby the teacher is in control at the front of the class, and all the students move along at the same pace) will generally only exacerbate the problems of mixed ability groups.

Underwood (1987) provides a wide range of activities which are particularly useful for mixed ability teachers to have in their repertoire.

Task: Complete the following questionnaire.

Classroom Management Questionnaire

Which of the following activities do you use regularly in your classes?

	YES	NO
1 All students listening to the teacher.	☐	☐
2 All students listening to recorded material.	☐	☐
3 Students repeating individually or chorally.	☐	☐
4 Individual students responding to the teacher.	☐	☐
5 Reading sections of the course-book:		
students, silently	☐	☐
teacher, out loud.	☐	☐
6 Students making notes (eg. of vocabulary) in notebooks.	☐	☐
7 Students completing written exercises individually.	☐	☐
8 Students working in pairs to complete written exercises.	☐	☐
9 Students doing oral practice in pairs.	☐	☐
10 Students solving problems in groups.	☐	☐
11 Students preparing their own material.	☐	☐
12 Stories, questions etc. in groups.	☐	☐
13 Group discussion of a topic.	☐	☐
14 Students completing tasks individually.	☐	☐

(Based on Underwood, 1987)

(See chapters 3 and 4 for more on classroom management and the role of the teacher).

ELT methodology: principled eclecticism

This is not a theoretical book, but it seems to me that one way of building teachers' awareness and self-assurance is to encourage them to relate theory to practice and practice to theory. In real terms, this means widening their knowledge of the options available to them, and sharpening their analysis of the principles underlying their teaching strategies. By these means, teachers will feel even better equipped to devise solutions to the problems that they understand better than anyone else, and to transfer the principles behind a successful activity to new situations, confident in their ability to recreate the initial success.

For these reasons, it is important for the mixed ability teacher to be familiar with the rich tradition of language teaching methodologies and be able to draw on its resources freely.

● We can learn from the grammar/translation approach that the mother tongue is a deep reservoir for learners to draw on.
● From the direct method, we learn to use the target language wherever possible.
● From the structural and audio-lingual approach, we have learnt to be more systematic about the formal properties of language and to give learners plenty of controlled practice.
● The communicative approach has reminded us of the obvious, that language is a tool for exchanging feelings and ideas and for getting people to do things.
● The humanistic approaches, such as the Silent Way and Suggestopedia, have reminded us that learners are individuals with feelings and thoughts of their own, and that 'physical and mental harmony is an important element because it takes into account the link between the body and the brain' *(Lawlor, 1988).*

I am in no way proposing a random approach: picking and choosing at whim from a hotch-potch of methodologies. Eclecticism, like the belief in one and only one method, must be principled. Selecting from a wide range of often contradictory approaches must be a rational process, informed by experience and a personal understanding of relevant theories. Thus, the best way of coping with a mixed ability class is to select what is most relevant to the particular needs of the learners, from the existing mosaic of ideas, materials and activities now available, while remaining realistic about what can be achieved in difficult circumstances, without adequate equipment or space.

Further reading

Brumfit, C. (1980) *Problems and Principles in English Teaching* (Pergamon)
Hemingway, P. (1986) 'Teaching a Mixed-Level Class' *(Practical English Teaching,* Vol. 7/1)
Lawlor, M. (1988) *Inner Track Learning* (Pilgrims)
Rinvolucri, M. (1986) 'Strategies for a Mixed Ability Group' *(Practical English Teaching,* Vol. 7/1)
Scheibl, R. (1984) 'Tips for Mixed Ability Classes' *(Practical English Teaching,* Vol. 4/4)
Underwood, M. (1987) *Effective Class Management* (Longman)

CHAPTER 2 | The 'good' language learner

In many large mixed ability groups, students have to develop a certain level of autonomy simply in order to survive. Teachers can only accord a limited degree of attention to any one student at any one time, and, in the mixed ability class, where the variety and discrepancy of individual needs is marked, the problem of competing (or not) for the teacher's attention can be quite acute. Students may go some way to solving it themselves, however, if they are able to identify their own needs and, wherever possible, to tackle these constructively and independently. When they are also able to communicate these needs effectively to their teacher as feedback, it can prove immensely useful in helping the teacher to target class activity firmly and specifically.

The main aim of this chapter is therefore practical: to suggest ways of training students to improve their strategies and thus increase their autonomy and efficiency as language learners. First, however, I would like to summarise some of the research which has been carried out on how the 'good' language learner learns. This research will then serve as the basis for practical suggestions for learner training that make up the large part of the chapter.

Although no one has yet come up with a definite profile of the 'good' language learner, there seems to be sufficient consensus for us to draw provisional conclusions and to make a start on systematically training our students to make fuller use of their potential to learn. An important point made by Rubin (1987) is that although some language learners are more successful than others, 'there will be several paths to success depending on the individual's learning style.' This is consistent with the mixed ability approach that consciously sets out to allow for individual differences in the way students tackle their learning objectives. Rubin goes on to make the following points about the good language learner.

- The learning process includes both explicit and implicit knowledge.
- Taking decisions about how they learn can help all types of learner to use their strategies more effectively.
- Weaker language learners can use successful strategies to improve their ability to learn.
- Teachers can promote successful learning strategies.
- Once taught to analyse their needs, students are the best judges of how to approach learning.
- Learner autonomy promotes more effective learning, both inside and outside the classroom.

- It is best to build on what the students already know.
- Active learners who internalise information by problem-solving learn more thoroughly.
- Human language use depends on both creative and critical faculties.
- The ability to monitor and evaluate one's own progress promotes more effective learning.

The implications of these principles are that a successful learner is active rather than passive, is able to reason and analyse, to make guesses and take risks. In addition to these 'cognitive processes', Rubin discusses 'communication strategies', which include the way in which a learner with limited knowledge of a language can enter into conversation with more fluent speakers and exploit the resources at his or her disposal in order to cope. Another strategy which allows exposure to natural language use and communication practice is what Rubin refers to as 'social strategy'.

Much of this is consistent with Krashen's concept of 'comprehensible input', where the learner is given the opportunity to understand messages in a 'low-anxiety situation'. What is particularly heartening for the mixed ability teacher is Krashen's insistence that the classroom is often the best place for students to get comprehensible input, as the level of language can be controlled and contextualised there to facilitate comprehension, and the atmosphere can be modified to encourage learning (see Krashen, 1982).

In an article tantalisingly called 'How to be a successful language learner' (1987), Anita Wenden reports the beliefs of students themselves:

- It is important to use the language in a natural context without worrying about mistakes.
- It is important to learn about the language (its grammar and vocabulary) and to learn from one's mistakes.
- Feelings are important: the learner must be stimulated and must not be ashamed to ask questions.
- Students must have a sense of self-esteem and must not feel humiliated.
- Some people have an aptitude for learning languages.

Task: Rank the following characteristics of the good language learner in order of importance, based on your own experience.

The 'good' language learner . . . | NUMBER |

1 is not afraid to experiment with the language.
2 is a good guesser.
3 is able to try out different ways of learning.
4 is a user of the language.
5 is aware of the language as a system.
6 is well organised.
7 sets him or herself realistic, short-term aims.
8 assesses and monitors his or her own progress regularly.
9 has a positive attitude towards language and learning.
10 is not afraid to make mistakes.

Learner training

What I would now like to do is to take some of these qualities and suggest some activities which will encourage learners to make more effective use of their own potential. 'Learner training' is based on the principle that students benefit not only from understanding the *content* of lessons (the 'what') but also from being made aware of the learning *process* (the 'how'). Most researchers also agree that a good learner is an independent learner – one, that is, who can carry on learning either when the teacher is absent or when their attention is focused elsewhere. The underlying aim of the exercises that follow is to create greater autonomy amongst learners, and thus equip them better for learning English in a large mixed ability group.

1 Self-assessment

Aim: to discuss and examine assessment criteria with the class; to promote learner independence and develop the students' evaluative capacity.

1 First, provide the class with the criteria you yourself use when you mark their work, and give them the opportunity to see how you would apply the criteria.
2 Discuss the criteria with the class, explaining any difficulties connected with them and giving examples from their own work (written, and – if possible – recorded).
3 Collect in their written homework and mark it, but write your comments and marks (if any) on a separate sheet of paper.
4 Give the students their homework back and ask them to mark it themselves and show you the result.
5 Give them your assessment to compare with their own.

Example criteria for written work

excellent	hardly any errors and no serious errors; natural, idiomatic English; well-connected.
very good	a few errors, one or two serious errors; accurate grammar and vocabulary; simple connectors.
good	a few serious errors: accurate but simple sentences; too few connectors.
borderline	basic sentences, mostly correct, but with fundamental and serious errors; meaning on the whole clear.
weak	not enough grammar and vocabulary for this topic; few connectors, mostly inaccurate; meaning often confused.

Comments
This approach is particularly appropriate in a mixed ability class as it provides guidance in areas where students may be lacking in confidence,

while offering them the challenge of 'being teacher' and thus encouraging them to take more responsibility for their own progress.

If you employ great discretion and sensitive timing, you might ask students to read each other's work and assess it using the criteria provided. Initially, students will probably choose to assess the work of people they consider to be of a similar language level to their own. However, as the students gain confidence, the pairs should be encouraged to mix and re-form, so that stronger students will have the opportunity to take a supportive and constructive attitude towards the less successful, and weaker students will be able to apply their assessment criteria to good work and benefit from what they see. Thus, one can turn mixed ability to the class's advantage and exploit difference in an interesting and positive way. (In such cases, the teacher can still take in homework and assess it. Students will be particularly interested to compare student and teacher assessments.)

2 Assessing the value of classroom activities

Aim: to elicit the students' opinion of the rationale behind class activities and their effectiveness, in order to encourage co-operation and understanding amongst the students.

1 After a pair-work activity (for example), give the students the following discussion points:

Do you agree or disagree with the following statements?

1 The task was useful.
2 The questions were easy.
3 The instructions were clear.
4 We made a lot of mistakes.
5 The activity was a waste of time.
6 It gave us the chance to use English.
7 The teacher did not have to do anything during the activity.

---

2 Give the students feedback on their response to the questionnaire, and discuss with them why they do pairwork (or any other student-centred activities). Gradually, as they begin to understand the benefit of these techniques, their attitude to them should become more positive. The exercise will also help the teacher in deciding how fast to introduce a more varied approach to learning, and in monitoring which students are having difficulty adjusting to new methods.

Comments

This technique can be applied to almost any activity in the classroom, from the teaching of grammar to the use of songs. It simply involves asking the students each time what they think the purpose of a particular exercise might be and how useful they find it.

3 Collective feedback

Aim: to increase the students' awareness of the methods and techniques adopted by the teacher to practise speaking and writing skills.

1 Groups discuss different aspects of the lesson or the course. For example, how do they feel about the amount of grammar they do in class? Is there too little or too much speaking practice? Do they feel they are learning enough new words? etc.
2 They keep notes of what is said in their discussion groups in order to exchange views with other groups and keep the teacher informed.
3 The teacher collects in this written work, reads and returns it, correcting errors of grammar and vocabulary in the process.
4 *(Optional)* The teacher blanks out some of the words in the texts before returning them to the students. The students then have a gap-filling text based on their own written summary of what was said in the group discussion. This is an example of 'learner-input' and is particularly useful in examination classes, where gap-filling is a regular activity.

Comments
Correcting the errors, and blanking out words from the students' final versions makes the activity a useful language-learning task (especially as it allows for anonymous feedback). It is above all, though, a consciousness-raising activity which explores the way the teacher is going about things and how the class feels about it. Here is an extract from one such written summary my students gave me (censored, of course!):

> Our group likes having discussions; we think conversation is the most important thing we do. We like the jokes and the stories.
> We want more grammar. We also want to learn more words. We want to know can we take the First Certificate in June.

Areas where the class as a whole is in agreement can be identified from such texts and can be written up as points on the board. This will give the teacher specific areas of need to address in future lessons, as well as a clearer idea of where further teaching and support are needed.

4 Is what we teach what they learn?

Aim: to check whether what the teacher intended to teach is, in fact, what the students think they learnt, and to give the students a greater awareness of the structure and aims of a (typical) lesson.

1 Ask the students to draft a lesson plan for a particular lesson you have taught. (This could be done as a group discussion, with different

groups focusing on different phases of the lesson and then exchanging ideas.)

2 To help them do this, you may wish to give them a framework similar to the following:

Phase 1: Presentation		
What the teacher did	What we did	Purpose of the activity

Phase 2: Practice		
What the teacher did	What we did	Purpose of the activity

3 Ask students to swop their completed charts with one another and spot the differences between them; they can report back on these! At the end of the lesson, collect in the worksheets and compare them with the aims you originally had in mind. If there are significant discrepancies, you should try to make your aims for future lessons more explicit. For example, this might involve more thorough checking procedures, or allowing more time to conclude at the end of a lesson.

5 Trying out different approaches

Aim: to make students more aware of their own learning processes, and so encourage them to try out *different* approaches to learning; to increase their learning efficiency where necessary.

1 Give the students a questionnaire to complete like the three given here. (With beginners, it can be in their mother tongue.)
2 Go through the first questions with the class as a whole and then ask students to continue on their own or working in pairs.
3 Discuss the results in a class feedback session and ask them to summarise their conclusions as written homework. When marking this work, you will be able to reconsider what action you should take to meet the students' needs and further their progress.

A

The Way I Learn English

1 What do you do when you find an unknown word in a text?
  a ask the teacher;
  b use my dictionary;
  c guess it if I can;
  d ask the person I'm sitting next to.

2 How do you note down new vocabulary?
a I write it in my textbook.
b I add it to a list in my notebook with a translation.
c I write it down in a group with similar words.
d I write it down with an example to show its meaning.

3 Which of the following do you find easiest?
a listening;
b speaking;
c reading;
d writing.

4 When you listen or read, do you ...
a try to understand everything?
b just try to answer the questions in the book?
c try to get the general idea first?
d use the context to get a better idea of what the text is about?

5 How do you like to learn grammar?
a by learning the rules first and then practising with examples;
b by doing exercises first and then working out the rules;
c by using the language to communicate;
d by comparing English with my own language.

6 How do you like to work in class?
a in pairs and groups;
b repeating what the teacher says all together;
c on my own;
d talking to the teacher.

7 When do you think the mother tongue should be used in class?
a never;
b to explain difficult words;
c to explain the grammar;
d when the teacher is giving instructions;

8 When you make a mistake, do you ...
a feel embarrassed?
b want the teacher to correct you every time?
c try to correct yourself?
d try to learn from the mistake?

9 Out of class, do you do any of the following?
a read English books and magazines;
b listen to songs in English;
c speak to people of other nationalities in English;
d write to your penfriend.

10 How do you feel about tests?
a They are very important.
b They are not necessary.
c They are a useful way of knowing if I have made progress.
d They make me work harder.

B

'How Often' Questionnaire

	OFTEN	SOMETIMES	NEVER
1 Do you ask the teacher when you don't understand a word?			
2 Do you use the mother tongue in class?			
3 Do you do well in tests?			
4 Do you speak English during group-work?			
5 Do you learn grammar rules by heart?			
6 Do you revise what you have done in class?			
7 Do you read English books outside class?			
8 Do you work out the rules of grammar on your own?			
9 Do you plan what you intend to learn in English?			
10 Do you check whether you have learnt what you planned to learn?			

C

Number the following 1–13 in order of importance to you as a learner:

	NUMBER
● Learning grammar rules	
● Talking to the teacher	
● Improving my pronunciation	
● Writing correctly	
● Talking to other students in English	
● Not making mistakes	
● Getting good marks in tests	
● Reading books in English	
● Writing down lots of new words	
● Finding out about life in English-speaking countries	
● Getting a certificate at the end of the course	
● Being able to express my ideas in English	
● Improving my professional qualifications	

6 Pictures of learning

Aim: as in the previous exercise.

1 Some students respond more readily to a visual stimulus than to words. The following diagrams are a very vivid and economical way of either introducing or ending a discussion on the way we learn. Ask the class to describe what they see in the pictures.

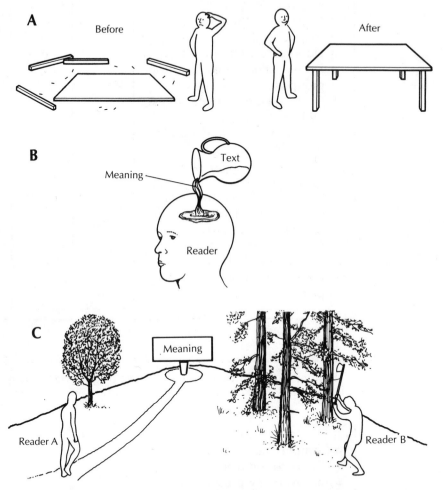

2 Then ask them to match the following statements with the pictures. They may choose more than one picture for each statement, if they wish, and different statements will apply to figures 1 and 2 in picture C.

1 The learner is passive.	6 Learning is easy.
2 The learner is active.	7 Learning is a jig-saw puzzle.
3 The learner knows a little.	8 Learning means thinking.
4 The teacher knows a lot.	9 Learning is boring.
5 Learning is hard work.	10 Learning is fun.

Comments
The first diagram illustrates a cognitive or problem-solving approach to learning. In this approach, the learner's role is an active one and involves them in thinking independently about how they learn. The second depicts the traditional learning situation, when the teacher is supposed to know everything and the students very little. The role of the student here is totally passive – he or she is treated as an empty receptacle. The third picture shows two learners, one of whom finds learning easy, the other of whom finds it very difficult and has to work hard to do well.

Possible answers: 1 B; 2 A; 3 B; 4 A; 5 C, R2; 6 C, R1; 7 A; 8 A; 9 B or C, R2; 10 A or C, R1.

These are not definitive answers. The important thing is to get students to discuss different possibilities and to say why they agree or disagree with you or each other.

The treatment of error

One of the most important aspects of learner training is that of encouraging the right attitude to error. It is essential to create an atmosphere in which errors can be accepted as a necessary step in the learning process. Errors can, for instance, actually raise awareness and reinforce a rule in a way that answers that are luckily correct cannot.

Many teachers, however, seem obsessed with eliminating mistakes and correct their students constantly. They perhaps feel safe doing this because it is an area in which they have authority and the students are vulnerable. This is probably particularly true of the large mixed ability class, where teachers often feel insecure about discipline and control. However, while correcting error is undoubtedly an important part of language teaching, there is an appropriate time and place for it, and while there are ways of correcting which encourage learners, there are also ways which discourage them. In a mixed ability class, this distinction is particularly important, as students are often tongue-tied not because they have nothing to say, but because they are afraid of being made to look foolish in front of other students by a teacher who pounces on their every mistake. An obsession with accuracy ('errorphobia') will thus often develop at the expense of fluency. Both accuracy and fluency are, of course, important, but a balance between them is vital. The grid on page 22 is given as a rough guide to when to focus on accuracy and the need to correct, and when to focus on fluency and the need for students to communicate using all the resources at their disposal.

There are a number of strategies the teacher can use to take the sting out of correction. Generally, one should try to get away from the solemnity and severity normally associated with correcting mistakes wherever possible. When marking work, for example, respond to the *content* of the students' oral or written work as well as the *form*. At the end of a composition on 'My Holidays', for instance, add a comment in response to the student's experiences – 'Sounds like you had a nice time'; 'What a disaster!'; 'Yes, but why didn't the travel agent book the

	PRESENTATION	PRACTICE	COMMUNICATION
focus on accuracy	✓	✓	
focus on form			✓
focus on meaning	✓	✓	✓
focus on use		(✓)	✓
immediate correction	✓	(✓)	
delayed correction			✓
teacher corrects	✓	✓	
learners correct (themselves, each other)			✓

hotels in advance?' etc. According to the same principle, if you are grading work or want to give an idea of the seriousness of individual mistakes, vary the conventional red ink and 'marks out of ten' approach with a lighter touch, such as funny faces:

a very good essay   not bad   bad   absolutely horrific

The following activities offer examples of how to make errors a positive learning experience, rather than something to be afraid of. It should be remembered, however, that highlighting students' individual strengths is as important as pointing out their mistakes. It is precisely in a mixed ability situation that students are likely to see their next-door neighbour succeed when they themselves are flagging, and it is under these circumstances that their self-esteem is most vulnerable. The mixed ability group, with its divergence of needs and its consequent tensions, too easily creates those conditions that isolate students and erode their confidence. Personal encouragement, and praise for specific achievements, can do much to compensate for this and can considerably boost the morale of the demotivated.

1 Spot the error

Aim: to encourage students to distinguish between minor and serious mistakes and to worry less about the former.

1 When marking students' homework, make a note of their errors and also of examples of correct language use. Mix up the correct and incorrect sentences and present them in random order on an OHP or the blackboard.

2 Show the sentences to the students and ask them to decide, in groups, whether the sentences are correct or incorrect. For each correct sentence, they should award a score of 3, for a small error a score of 2, and for a serious error a score of 1. Explain that a serious error is one which actually changes the meaning and/or seriously obstructs communication, and that a minor error expresses the essential meaning but in an awkward or clumsy manner.

Here are some examples of correct and incorrect student sentences and their possible scores. (These scores may in fact vary slightly from group to group, according to language level, age group, and so on.)

1 I like reading my bicycle.	2
2 I spend money for buying cigarettes.	2
3 I like classical music.	3
4 I like very much the volley.	2
5 The cooker is an excellent one.	2
6 I'm interested in music.	3
7 They have chairs in their hands.	1
8 I have great agony waiting for the bus.	1
9 Films can make you amuse.	1/2
10 I've bought this yesterday.	2

Comments

The range of sentences selected for this exercise ensures that students are made aware of what they can do well, as well as their weaknesses. Some students will recognise their errors, but they won't lose face as the whole process is anonymous. Discussion should arise on how serious or not any one error is. This will offer the opportunity to clarify certain issues afresh.

2 Classifying errors

Aim: to help both the teacher and learner think more systematically about the types of error that are being committed in the group and thus learn from them; to provide the learner with a useful record of typical mistakes.

1 Prepare a sheet like the following for recording errors:

FORM	MEANING	USE	PRONUNCIATION	STUDENT

2 During the communicative phase of a lesson, go round the class listening in (discreetly!) to what the students are saying. Note down their errors in the appropriate categories on the sheet and also note down which students made which errors.
- Errors of *form* are grammatical errors.
- Errors of *meaning* may result from a vocabulary mistake, but can also occur when a grammatical form is used wrongly: 'I will leave in five minutes' is grammatically correct, but may have required the Present Continuous tense in the context.
- Errors of *use* are communicative errors, where the grammar and basic meaning are correct, but the register or tone is inappropriate to the context. ('Give me some beer' is perfectly correct, for example, but in a pub or when visiting a friend, it would be considered impolite; one makes a polite request by saying something like 'I'd like a drink,' or 'Could I have a drink/a pint of beer,' or by adding 'please' with the appropriate intonation.)
- Errors of *pronunciation* may include mispronunciation of individual sounds and also inappropriate intonation.

3 When the communicative activity or discussion phase is over, offer the students feedback on some of their errors using your chart. Take care not to say which students made which errors.

4 Ask the students to copy the error-category columns of your chart and to put the errors you read out in the appropriate columns. Tell them, or elicit from them, the correct version first. Alternatively, you could just write the errors on the board in random order and allow students to work on their own or with a partner to classify them using the chart. Go round helping weaker students while the class is working on this task, and take the opportunity to discuss their individual errors with them.

3 Noughts and crosses

Aim: to consolidate language points and correct error in a lively and motivating manner. This game can be played at a very simple level or a more complex one, depending on individual abilities. It is a good example of 'teacher-made' material which suits specific needs.

1 Draw a box like the following one on the board:

2 The two teams – noughts (0) and crosses (X) – have to try and complete a horizontal, vertical or diagonal row of noughts or crosses by taking it in turns to come to the front and fill in one of the boxes. A completed grid might look like this:

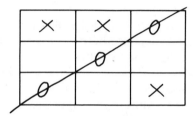

3 Draw another grid, but this time filled with a selection of correct and incorrect sentences from the students' homework:

1 HE IS INTO THE SHOP	2 I RIDE A BOOK	3 I LIKE VERY MUCH MUSIC
4 I LIKE GOING TO THE CINEMA	5 I AM STUDENT	6 JOHN PLAYS THE GUITAR
7 I AM INTERESTED FOR MUSIC	8 I LIVE IN A FLAT	9 SHE SHOOK MY ARM

4 Ask the students to copy the grid into their notebooks, but leaving the boxes blank.

5 Give the class a few minutes to decide which sentences are correct and incorrect.

6 Divide the class into two teams (noughts and crosses).

7 Explain that each team has to try and complete a row of boxes with noughts or crosses, as before. To do this, they have to say whether the sentences in the boxes are right or wrong and, if wrong, to provide the correct version. (When I do this, I start the game off by asking teams a general knowledge question. I also stop the game at critical moments or when one side commits a foul (for example, using their mother tongue or making a serious linguistic error) and ask a general knowledge question).

8 When the game is over, ask the students to copy the correct sentences into their books in grid-form. Association with the pleasurable experience of the game should make the correct language easier to remember later.

Comments

I first encountered a version of 'noughts and crosses' for language teaching in Rinvolucri (1982). There are other ludic activities for dealing with error, such as the board-game 'snakes and ladders', but this is one of the easiest to implement with a large mixed ability class.

Towards learner autonomy

There are many aspects of good language learning that I have not been able to illustrate here, so I would like to conclude this chapter with a checklist of ideas which may guide learners towards greater autonomy. It may be useful to give the checklist to your students as a handout to remind them of ways in which they can increase their autonomy as learners. Most of the suggestions in the checklist are based on observing my own pupils over a number of years; others are drawn from the extensive range of 'good learner' texts now available.

Learner Autonomy: A Checklist

1 Make a list of the things you intend to learn on your language course.
2 At the end of each term, check how many of your aims you have fulfilled.
3 Write down how you think you learnt your mother tongue or another foreign language.
4 Keep a diary of how your learning is progressing; for example, 'things I learnt today', 'things I found difficult' or 'books I have read'.
5 Read as much as you can in your own time: simplified readers, magazines – anything. Keep a list of everything you read in English.
6 Copy down examples of English you see around you every day; for example, signs, notices, advertisements, the 'blurb' on books or packages in shops, etc.
7 Record new vocabulary systematically, by topic or alphabetically, in a separate notebook or looseleaf binder.
8 Build up your own grammar in a separate notebook, alphabetically, and add memorable, personal or humorous examples whenever you come across them.
9 Keep all your written assignments in a folder, and at the end of term, make a list of all your most frequent errors.
10 Find a penfriend and write to them as regularly as you can. (Have you thought of the possibility of a cassette friend?)
11 If you like pop songs, listen to them carefully and write down the words.
12 Keep a notebook of famous quotations or memorable things said in English, from your reading of literature or newspapers, or from hearsay. (Jokes are, in fact, a good place to start.)
13 Get a good dictionary, and if there is a workbook to go with it, work through some of the exercises.
14 Assess your ability in different skills, such as listening, speaking, reading, writing, vocabulary and grammar. Mark yourself on a scale of 1 to 5, and decide which areas you must concentrate on.

---

15 Listen to the news in English if you have access to the BBC World Service or some other English language radio programme. Then listen to the news in your own language and check how much you understood.
16 Make a list of all the different kinds of texts people read, either in their mother tongue or in a foreign language. Do they read them all in the same way? Which, for example, do they read slowly, which fast?
17 Record yourself reading a text in English: play it back and think how it compares with a native-speaker reader. How could you improve the reading? Try re-recording yourself.
18 Write down the advantages and disadvantages of group-work in the classroom.
19 How many English words do you know that are similar to their equivalents in your language? Write them down. Can you name some of the obvious differences between your language and English?
20 Think of one more thing you can do to help yourself become a more independent learner.

Further reading

Bertoldi, E., J. Kollar and E. Richard (1988) 'Learning How to Learn English' (*English Language Teaching Journal*, Vol. 42/3)

Ellis, G. and B. Sinclair (1990) *Learning to Learn English* (Cambridge University Press)

Porte, G. (1988) 'Poor Language Learners and Their Strategies for Dealing with New Vocabulary' (*English Language Teaching Journal*, Vol. 42/3)

Rinvolucri, M. (1984) *Grammar Games* (Cambridge University Press)

Rubin, J. (1987) 'What the Good Language Learner Can Teach Us' (*TESOL Quarterly*, 9/1)

Stern, H. H. (1983) *Fundamental Concepts of Language Teaching* (Oxford University Press)

Wenden A. and J. Rubin (eds.) (1987) *Learner Strategies in Language Learning* (Prentice-Hall)

CHAPTER 3 | The role of the teacher

Task: Which of the following have you heard teachers say?

1 'They just don't want to learn.'
2 'There's one that just comes to make trouble.'
3 'They can't even read in their own language, never mind in English.'
4 'Nothing I do works with that class.'
5 'A few trouble-makers spoil it for all those who really want to learn.'
6 'They're just not interested in English.'
7 'The only way I can get them to shut up is by giving them a test.'
8 'I do choral repetition because that way I'm in control.'
9 'They just laugh and make a lot of noise if we do group-work.'
10 'If I'm friendly with them, they just take advantage.'

How many of the statements indicate that there may be something the teacher could do to improve the situation?

In talking to teachers of mixed ability groups over the years about seemingly insoluble classroom problems (lack of motivation being at the top of the blacklist), I have come to feel that the problem lies as much with the teachers' attitudes as it does with their students. Teaching large mixed ability classes is no soft option and, all too often, teachers can lose faith in their students' desire to learn. In effect, this often means a loss of confidence in their own ability to motivate students, and it is the unmotivated or insecure learner in the group who will inevitably suffer most. This is no easy matter, and while the later chapters of this book *do* put forward specific techniques which the desperate teacher can put into immediate practice, they will offer no more than superficial solutions unless he or she embarks on a process of personal and professional development.

For although we should do all we can to encourage good learning techniques amongst our students, one must assume that there is a limit to how far we can change the nature of those who come to our classes. On the other hand, there is a great deal we can do to change *our own* role, redefining it, and thinking of ways of opening it up, extending and varying it. It is in this way that a teacher can bring out the underlying strength in each and every one of their students, by building up their own confidence and professional skills.

Situation and personality: the 'SWOT' test

If we are to open the way towards a more challenging and therefore satisfying role for the teacher, we should be both realistic about the obstacles in our way and positive about the opportunities we can make available. The ultimate objective will be to improve the teacher's self-image and widen the range of roles available to him or her. The SWOT test is a convenient framework in which to do this. A SWOT test requires us to look at a particular situation in terms of Strengths, Weaknesses, Opportunities and Threats. So far, this book has addressed itself to both native and non-native-speaking teachers of English. In this section, however, I would like to apply the SWOT test to a 'worst possible' mixed ability scenario in order to confront the problems as realistically as I can. For this purpose, I will take as an example the case of the non-native-speaking teacher faced with a large mixed ability class in difficult circumstances.

S = Strengths
The non-native-speaking teacher has several advantages over their native-speaker counterpart when teaching a mixed ability class in difficult circumstances. Amongst these are the following:
- knowledge of the students' mother tongue – an enormous and neglected resource for the hard-pressed language teacher;
- knowledge of the students' culture – invaluable both in terms of rapport and as a source of strategies for motivating reluctant learners;
- first-hand knowledge of the students' preferred learning styles – a solid basis on which to build learner-training exercises (see chapter 2);
- a detailed and systematic knowledge of English grammar – an important aspect of any language system and invaluable in teaching communication in a coherent manner;
- knowledge of the learners' previous educational experience and its possible influence on their attitude to learning English;
- (with learners of school age) knowledge of other subjects in the school curriculum and an awareness of how these subjects may be exploited in the foreign language classroom.

> **Task:** Think of one other advantage of non-native-speaking teacher may have over a native-speaker.

Comments
I have deliberately chosen to begin by listing some of the redeeming features of teaching in difficult circumstances because it is an important first step for teachers faced with an apparently hopeless situation to think positively and creatively about it. The only way out of an apparent dead-end is to discover the potential of previously unsuspected resources.

W = weaknesses

Non-native-speaking teachers are often particularly pessimistic about their own teaching potential. Some of the reasons they identify for this feeling of inadequacy are as follows:

- a lack of confidence with the language (there can sometimes be students in the class whose English is as good, if not better, than theirs);
- a lack of training in techniques and methodology (university studies are often based on linguistics and literature, and offer little or no teaching practice as part of the course);
- mixed ability groups, which are difficult to teach at the best of times, but acutely difficult for an inadequately trained non-native speaker;
- large classes;
- the low prestige of English studies in the national curriculum, and a consequent lack of interest in the subject on the part of students;
- a lack of equipment (perhaps no OHP or school cassette recorder – although these are often to be found locked away in a cupboard, gathering dust!);
- textbooks that are unsuitable for the students' needs;
- having to share a classroom with other teachers;
- students' obsession with marks, and passing tests and examinations;
- family responsibilities at home which leave little time available for the preparation of lessons;

and

- the low esteem in which women teachers may be held, and consequent discipline problems.

Task: Tick those of the above points which apply to you, and then think of one other problem you face in your teaching situation:

Comments

I have tried to take a particularly bleak view of the circumstances in which many language teachers have to do their job. One hopes things are not this bad for most of them, but one fears they may be for many. The suggestions I make in this book try and take these circumstances into account; for the most part, supplementary activities must be realistic in their aims, simple to prepare, and have maximum effect in terms of language acquisition and production. This does not suggest we should take a defeatist attitude towards what is possible; our view of both the learner and the teacher must be one of potential for growth.

In this chapter, I will focus on what teachers can do in both the short-term and long-term to make their role more effective, and to adapt that role to the needs of the learners in a mixed ability class. This will largely be a matter of increasing the range of options available to them, and of identifying existing opportunities that are perhaps not so obvious.

O = Opportunities

Even less research has been carried out on the 'good' language teacher than on the successful language learner, so we are to some extent guessing as to why it is that some teachers seem able to facilitate the learning process, which others do not (see Harmer, 1983). Of course, the teacher is only one factor in the teaching situation, and not always the most decisive. Nevertheless, the teacher's role and what makes it effective are relevant to any discussion of mixed ability teaching. Certainly, the term 'good' is a very relative one. The 'good' teacher should be able to adapt his or her style and range of activities to suit individual needs, no matter how large or mixed a group is. Thus, 'good' must be seen, not as a finite term, but one needing infinite interpretations.

Here are the results of a survey carried out with forty language learners to find out what *they* thought made a good language teacher. These learners were of Cambridge First Certificate or Proficiency level so we can assume that they were themselves reasonably successful learners. The survey took the form of an interview in which students were asked to recall their favourite and least favourite teachers, and to say why they thought some teachers were better than others. Below is a summary of what they said about their favourite teachers. (These transcriptions have only been corrected where language errors have obscured the intended meaning.)

Task: As you read the chart, tick those opportunities for good teaching which you have already developed in yourself, and those you feel you could develop in the future.

Qualities of a good teacher	NOW	FUTURE
1 friendly		
2 explained things		
3 gave good notes		
4 knew how to treat someone who sits at a desk for six hours		
5 let the students do it by themselves in groups		
6 We did the lesson together.		
7 got out of us the things we know		
8 talked about her life		
9 talked about problems of the school		
10 talked about other subjects		
11 played games		
12 told jokes		
13 She was one of us.		
14 didn't push weak learners		
15 asked students opinions, there was a dialogue		
16 She was like an actress; she pretended a lot.		

17 She was forceful, but not strict. ☐ ☐
18 She was educated. ☐ ☐
19 She knew psychology. ☐ ☐
20 used movement to make meaning clear ☐ ☐
21 She made sure everyone understood. ☐ ☐
22 She was funny. ☐ ☐
23 read in a tone that made meaning clear ☐ ☐
24 She got close to students. ☐ ☐
25 believed in me, made me believe in myself ☐ ☐
26 I wanted him to be proud of me. ☐ ☐
27 He had a personality of his own. ☐ ☐
28 She was very experienced. ☐ ☐
29 She made grammar clear. ☐ ☐
30 They tried to communicate. ☐ ☐
31 She gave advice. ☐ ☐
32 He talked about personal problems. ☐ ☐
33 She gave me a lot of books to read. ☐ ☐
34 She used questions a lot. ☐ ☐
35 She asked all the students questions. ☐ ☐
36 social work – it was their job ☐ ☐
37 We cut up animals. [i.e. did experiments/
    practical work!] ☐ ☐
38 talked about the lesson ☐ ☐
39 She knew mathematics. [i.e. her subject] ☐ ☐
40 She was more like a comedian. ☐ ☐

Comments
This list of qualities is long and the individual items are in no particular order of priority. This has its advantages: it highlights the fact that many different and contradictory qualities can contribute to effective teaching. It is actually encouraging that students do not come up with a single, consistent picture of the ideal teacher. To be prescriptive about this would assume a greater understanding of the learning process than we in fact have and would probably limit our flexibility and creativity. In the mixed ability classroom, we have to cater for very many different learning tastes and aptitudes, and we must try to remain as receptive as possible to new openings and opportunities for development. The teacher who depends on a certain few formulaic solutions to every new challenge that arises will often be both demotivated and demotivating. (See Harmer, 1983, if you are interested in the results of another survey on what makes a good language teacher.)

T = threats

The things teachers do to make their lives more difficult are many and varied! Moreover, what students have to say about bad teaching is as inconsistent as their comments on good teaching. Their opinions are, nevertheless, a good place to start.

Below is a summary of the negative characteristics a group of students highlighted when discussing teachers they thought taught badly.

Task: Although you may not agree with their views, tick those features of teaching style which may apply to you, and tick in the second column if you think that by changing that aspect of your teaching, you might improve it.

Characteristics of a poor teacher

	TRUE OF NOW	WORTH CHANGING
1 very strict	☐	☐
2 didn't let us speak	☐	☐
3 gave us a text to learn and checked it	☐	☐
4 gave marks all the time	☐	☐
5 She was fixed in a chair.	☐	☐
6 He had favourite students.	☐	☐
7 always above our heads	☐	☐
8 shouted for no reason	☐	☐
9 gave a lot of tests	☐	☐
10 forced us to do things	☐	☐
11 didn't discuss other problems	☐	☐
12 started the lesson immediately	☐	☐
13 didn't smile	☐	☐
14 She stared at you and you couldn't say a word even if you wanted to.	☐	☐
15 His tests were too difficult.	☐	☐
16 We were not prepared for the test.	☐	☐
17 He just showed us a grammar rule and we forgot it.	☐	☐
18 shouted when we made mistakes	☐	☐
19 very nervous	☐	☐
20 talked and talked	☐	☐
21 she spoke flat	☐	☐
22 She just said the lesson and nothing else.	☐	☐
23 There was a distance from us.	☐	☐
24 believed that students were all the same	☐	☐
25 We didn't do experiments. [practical things]	☐	☐

26 believed students all knew the same things	☐	☐
27 like a machine	☐	☐
28 not prepared	☐	☐
29 treated kids like objects	☐	☐
30 She was rigid.	☐	☐
31 sarcastic and ironic	☐	☐
32 only lessons – didn't discuss anything else	☐	☐
33 avoided answering questions	☐	☐
34 You couldn't laugh, you couldn't speak.	☐	☐
35 He was the teacher, I was the student.	☐	☐
36 He had a blacklist and said, 'You, you, you.'	☐	☐
37 She had a little book with the marks in.	☐	☐
38 no communication, nothing	☐	☐
39 She made me feel anxious.	☐	☐
40 He said we weren't well prepared.	☐	☐

Comments

The diversity of opinion expressed above over what constitutes effective teaching would seem to confirm the assumption that there are no set formulae and that very different personalities can make good teachers for different reasons. My own experience of observing teachers at work over the years suggests that introverts and extroverts, soft-spoken and outspoken people, theatrical and non-theatrical types, can all hold the attention of a class and make learning enjoyable and effective.

It would, however, be both defeatist and counterproductive not to pick out certain general principles that are often shared by good teachers. These may act as a starting-point for teachers who have lost confidence in their own potential. Figure 1 opposite summarises some of the salient patterns to be drawn from the comments made by students in response to my survey. It shows how the teacher can get trapped within certain constraints which, when overcome, will activate a much wider range of roles. It would be worthwhile discussing some of these areas in further detail.

The voice of authority

One of the areas of constraint frequently to be found in the restrictive inner circle is that of teacher authority. As discussed earlier, this is often asserted over a difficult class by adopting a testing, rather than teaching, approach to language learning. Power lies in the teacher's dispensing of marks and in the detection and penalisation of error. This privilege

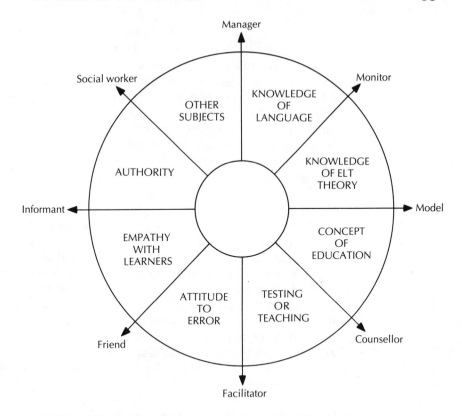

Figure 1

TESTING emphasises:	TEACHING emphasises
failure	success
correctness	appropriacy
impersonality	personalisation
anxiety	pleasure
marks	results
boring, mechanical content	interesting, flexible content
judgement	support
extrinsic motivation	intrinsic motivation
competition	co-operation
teacher control	student control

Task: Add the following terms to the appropriate column above:

integration, division, incentive, threat, humour, po-faced solemnity, give and take, crime and punishment, end product, process.

Figure 2

of power may lessen the symptoms of insecurity in the teacher, but it raises anxiety levels amongst students in the class.

The failure to distinguish between testing and teaching is a major obstacle to the effective handling of the mixed ability class. Both these processes are essential in language learning, but it is vital to distinguish between them, and to use testing – whether formal or informal – judiciously. The summary on page 35 (Figure 2) shows the main differences between the two, and should go some way towards explaining how crucial a positive and holistic approach is in uniting and motivating a mixed ability group.

Comments

It will be seen that many of the points raised by students in the second part of the survey described in this chapter come up in the testing column above. The features in the testing column cannot be transformed into those in the teaching column from one day to the next, but the teacher could, for instance, start by moving away from an approach based on the formula 'text + questions'. It is asking for trouble to have the class listen to or read a text (particularly a boring one at that!) and then plod through the comprehension questions, which often do not do what they are supposed to anyway, i.e. test comprehension!

To get a feel of the 'text + questions' approach from the students' point of view, try this exercise:

Task: Read the text and answer the questions that follow.

The pringle squiggled down the road.
It koshed the scrob because it dingled.

1 Did the pringle squiggle?
2 Did it squiggle down the mountain?
3 Where did the pringle squiggle?
4 What did it do to the scrob?
5 Why did it do that?

How many questions did you get right? Did you make any mistakes? Did you understand the text? Did the comprehension questions test comprehension?

Teachers who feel insecure and under pressure often look to the experts to provide solutions. The expert becomes a guru or magician who can solve our problems for us with a simple formula; if only we could learn their secret, all our problems would disappear and our students would respond in lessontime exactly as we want them to. I said earlier that there are no recipes for success, and equally, there are no secret formulae. If there were, we could set about learning the mechanical principles of successful teaching like a child with a box of tricks and a set of instructions. Instead, we must learn to create our own personal magic of a more ordinary kind. A teacher's relationships with individual students and different classes will always be unique, and these are crucial to the success of the teaching process. Given how vital and special a role personal interaction plays in the classroom, it would therefore be insulting to try and repeat the same tricks indefinitely as though the teacher-pupil relationship were not going to change and evolve. It is in this respect that a knowledge of language-teaching theory can be seen as an important force, despite the widely-held belief that it is sterile, boring, or a waste of time compared to personal practice and experience. A sound theoretical knowledge can prove invaluable in helping teachers to contextualise and objectivise their relationships with classes. It can deepen their understanding of the problems they come up against in the classroom and help them to generate new ideas and techniques in a principled fashion rather than an ad hoc way. It serves to widen teachers' choices and can revitalise their personal pedagogical viewpoint.

In a time of rapid social change, language-teaching theory is throwing up a profusion of approaches and methods to cope with the plurality of needs in a modern technological world. This is healthy, as it widens the choices available to the hard-pressed teacher; but it can be difficult to keep a sense of perspective on past and present, as old methods are rejected for new, often for no genuine practical reason. Knowledge of ELT history and practice means not only knowing about a wide range of methods and techniques, past and present, but knowing when to have them ready at your finger tips in order to use them. An ELT professional should know at least what the following approaches have to offer and the principles behind them (if only to reject them, in part or wholesale).

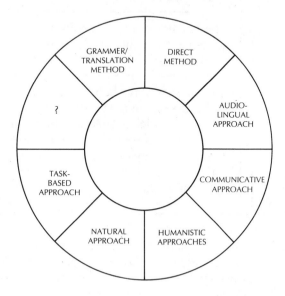

The liberated teacher

Having broken out of the inner circle of professional and pedagogic constraints, teachers will find themselves with many parts to play: friend, manager, monitor, counsellor, facilitator of learning, reliable informant on the language, social worker, model for the students, and so on.

Task: The chart below describes some of the things teachers do. Write down the role you think the teacher is performing in each case.

ACTIVITY	ROLE(S)
The teacher gives instructions for students to get into groups.	
The teacher asks students to repeat a sentence after him/her for pronunciation practice.	
The teacher goes round listening to pairs practising a dialogue.	
The teacher advises students how best to approach a task.	
The teacher explains when we use the Present Perfect for recently completed actions.	
The teacher provides material and guidance to enable students to work on their own.	
The teacher stays behind after class to discuss one of the students' personal problems, which is affecting their work.	
The teacher chats to students over coffee or arranges a cinema visit with the class.	

There are many more roles for the teacher than those listed here, and there is much more to these roles than the hints I have given in the table above (see Harmer, 1983; Nolasco and Arthur, 1988). My main purpose has been to emphasise the importance of adopting a wide variety of roles as opposed to the same two or three (in the traditional classroom, usually those of controller of activities, presenter of information and assessor of correctness or error). We will only begin to fathom the complexities of the mixed ability classroom when we can implement a sensitive and flexible methodology, in a perceptive way.

Further reading

Bartram, B. and R. Walton (1991) *Correction* (Language Teaching Publications)

Edge, J. (1990) *Mistakes and Correction* (Longman)

Harmer, J. (1983) *The Practice of English Language Teaching* (Longman)

Stern, H. H. (1983) *Fundamental Concepts of Language Teaching* (Oxford University Press) (See pp. 419–573.)

Wright, T. (1987) *Roles of Teachers and Learners* (Oxford University Press)

I.A.T.E.F.L. (for further information on teacher development):
3 Kingsdown Chambers
Kingdown Park
Tankerton
Whitstable
Kent C15 2DJ
UK

T.E.S.O.L. also has branches in many countries.

CHAPTER 4 | Keeping the class together

Teacher: I wish you'd pay a little attention, Smith!
Pupil: I'm paying as little as I can, sir.

One of the most common problems of the large mixed ability class is cohesion. This is an area that is governed not so much by *what* the teacher is doing, as *how* he or she is doing it; that is to say, it is not necessarily the content of the lesson (linguistic or thematic) that engages or alienates a class, but the way the content is being presented and practised. This chapter deals with the importance of classroom management in shaping the dynamics of a mixed ability lesson. Classroom management encompasses the decisions we make concerning our use of space and time: where we stand and who we look at; the way we ask questions and check understanding; the way we use our voice. Many of these skills are neglected areas in a teacher's training; yet they are often the reason why lessons fail, especially in large mixed ability classes where the sheer disparity of the students' language level and interests can prove a strongly divisive influence. The larger the class, or the more mixed the ability of the students in it, the more easily the lesson will seem to disintegrate.

The following diagram shows some reasons why a lesson might fall apart:

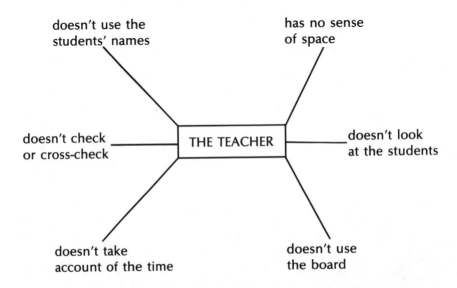

doesn't use the
students' names

has no sense
of space

doesn't check
or cross-check

THE TEACHER

doesn't look
at the students

doesn't take
account of the time

doesn't use
the board

Because of the different levels in a mixed ability group, it is difficult to keep the attention of all the students at the same time; what is interesting and challenging for one learner may be boring or too easy for another. So while the teacher's attention is fixed on one side of the class, the other side may begin to lose concentration, switch off and get increasingly noisy. Before long, the class can be in fragments.

In this section, I would like to put some detail on the diagram above by focusing on those aspects of classroom management that are particularly important in a mixed ability class, which is by definition composed of differences. The use of space and time, of students' names, eye contact, or the blackboard, and the ways in which checking is conducted, all contribute to the cohesion of a lesson or the 'togetherness' of a group of students.

The open space

A lot of classrooms traditionally look something like this:

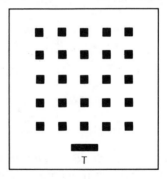

This is distinctly militaristic – fine for drilling and testing, but too rigid and uniform for real flexibility and variety. In many classes, there is little the teacher can do by way of rearranging the desks, either because there are too many of them or because they are screwed to the floor. Wherever possible, however, the space should be used in ways that encourage students to listen to each other and enable the maximum number at any one time to see the board or any visual material the teacher may be holding up. For general classwork, a semi-circular formation is normally best for this.

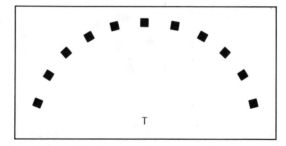

For general discussion, a circle can be formed, with the teacher either joining in as an equal in the discussion, or sitting just outside it to monitor what goes on or whisper suggestions to students trying to express themselves but at a loss for words.

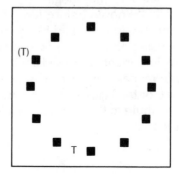

In a large class where the desks are fixed to the floor, students should be encouraged to work with people behind or in front of them or across a gangway, forming groups of four, six or nine.

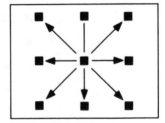

Even if the desks are immovable, the same cannot be said for the teacher, whose movement round the room at different points in the lesson can have a significant effect on the concentration of the students. Certainly, barricading oneself behind a desk for most of the lesson, and for most lessons, not only ignores the dynamics of the open space, but invites apathy and lack of involvement in the learners too. On the other hand, teachers can often go up close to students when they are speaking, and thus actually exclude the rest of the class from what's going on, particularly when the teacher turns their back on them as well:

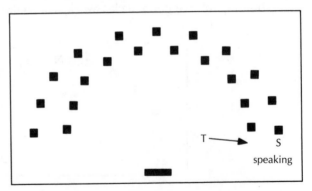

In addition, if a student's voice is not audible from the other end of the room, those students who are unable to hear will get irritated or just stop listening. In the illustrations below, the teacher's position encourages the student with a soft voice to speak up, while allowing the teacher to keep an eye on a maximum number of learners simultaneously and to focus their attention on the student speaking, or on the board or visual aids.

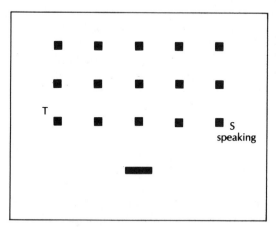
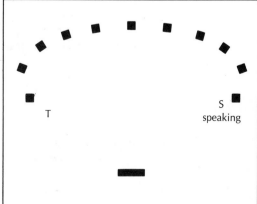

Time: friend or enemy?

If we remind ourselves of how important time is in our everyday lives, we may be surprised at the way we try and ignore its presence in the classroom. Time is invisible, but ubiquitous; when we overlook it, it makes its presence felt in sometimes disastrous ways. In a mixed ability class, time is particularly significant because learners sometimes differ not so much in knowledge as in concentration span or the speed in which they are likely to apply their knowlege. Moreover, when the teacher is trying to prevent a large mixed ability class from falling apart, time can have an important cohesive role.

Ten Ways of Taking Time into Account

1 Don't plan to do too much in a lesson. Have an 'extra' such as an anecdote or joke in reserve rather than cram the lesson with elaborate activities.
2 Tell your students at the start of each lesson roughly what you intend to do and how long it's going to take.
3 Tell them how long they have for a particular activity.
4 Warn the class one or two minutes before an activity is due to finish.
5 Use the last few minutes of the lesson to check what has been learned and to summarise what the lesson's targets have been.

6 Allow your students time to copy important information from the board before you rub it all off, particularly at the end of the lesson.

7 Give 'slower' students time to answer your questions or to present the results of a task before you move on to another student.

8 Don't, however, wait *too* long for a student to answer, as this breaks the lesson and it may be difficult to pick up momentum again.

9 If you forget your watch, borrow one of the students'.

10 Vary the timing and pacing of activities to build up a sense of rhythm in the lesson and give it shape. Alternate short, light interludes with longer phases of more intense activity.

Cross-checking

Attention in a large mixed ability class can be focused and held if the teacher follows a simple routine for involving students in what their fellow students are saying. The technique is one of 'cross-checking'. This involves checking a response given by one student with that of other students in a different part of the classroom. This is especially useful when particular students are struggling to express themselves, and others in the class have stopped listening.

There are specific points in the lesson when this is likely to happen. Imagine a phase of a lesson in which the students are doing any of the following:

● answering comprehension questions;
● suggesting words to fill in the blanks in a text;
● reporting the results of pair- or group-work;
● presenting the results of pair- or group-work in the form of a dialogue;
● asking the teacher to explain a point of grammar or vocabulary;
● asking the teacher to clarify instructions for a task;
● discussing a topic arising from a reading text.

Students are used to thinking that the teacher is the only person worth listening to in class, and that the only reason why the teacher asks questions of a particular student is to check up on them. As a result, they switch off unless the teacher asks them a question. This is all the more true when the student speaking happens to have acquired a reputation for contributing nothing but mistakes to the lesson.

Over a period of time, new habits can be encouraged if the teacher elicits responses from other students to something one of them has said or asked. This will not only focus attention and encourage involvement (particularly on the part of more advanced students who tend to get bored easily), but, in so doing, it should reduce discipline problems too. For example, when a student answers a comprehension question, ask someone else: 'Do you agree?' or 'What do you think, [John]?' Similarly, before a student or group presents the results of a task, ask the rest of the class to listen and say if they agree or not; ask them to see if they get the same answers, or, more specifically, to name one difference, if there is one, between their own answers and those of the student speaking. (In this approach, different groups may correct each other not so much by mistake-spotting, which can be destructive and demoralising, but through a more open response to the content of other students' presentations). When a student has asked or answered a question, get someone else to repeat what they have said, by saying, 'Sorry, I didn't hear that. What did he/she say, [Sarah]?' (The teacher's pretended deafness adds humour to the lesson as well as getting students used to listening to each other.) Finally, when students work in pairs, make reporting back to the class afterwards a matter of routine. Reporting back the answers their partners have given, and not only their own, will encourage them to complete pair-work activities.

The position of the teacher in the room during the cross-checking phases of the lesson should vary according to who he or she has addressed a comment or question to. Discreetly move away from the student who is speaking or about to speak, so that your field of control is defined and extended by your voice (directing questions or comments to different areas of the class); by your position (alerting students who might otherwise feel at a safe distance); and by eye contact (most of the class should be within view for most of the time).

The power of the written word

Wherever appropriate, pair-work should involve written answers, even if only in note-form. This has a number of advantages in the mixed ability class:

- It encourages reluctant learners to complete the task. (The end-product is a record of work done or not done.)
- It discourages them from using only the mother tongue, as they learn to expect a feedback phase in English.
- It gives faster students more to do while you go round helping slower students.
- It gives the teacher something concrete to discuss with early finishers. (When the task is purely oral, you soon get fast learners sitting back, twiddling their thumbs, claiming to have nothing more to do.)
- The checking and cross-checking process has a greater chance of success than if students have got nothing to refer to when they dry up.

If techniques such as these are to have an impact on the cohesion of the mixed ability class, the teacher will have to train the students over a period of time to ask as well as answer questions, and to learn to interact with each other, not only with the teacher. Paying attention to others and interacting with them should become a normal, classroom routine, rather than be saved up for a communicative or 'speaking' phase of a lesson.

Nominating

Use your students' names when eliciting answers or information and when checking. Using names makes for better rapport with students, and involves them directly and rapidly when need be. Although it is a good idea to allow them time to think and volunteer an answer to questions, if you wait too long sometimes, the momentum is lost and boredom can begin to set in. An over-reliance on volunteers to speak will degenerate into a show dominated by the most confident or extrovert students. However, an equal distribution of questions is difficult to achieve without the systematic, and encouraging, use of students' names.

Eye contact or star-gazing?

Why is eye contact considered to be so important in interaction between people? Try this experiment: when a friend of yours is speaking to you, look away, avoiding eye contact with them. How do they react? Similarly, how do you react if someone is telling you something but is looking over your shoulder or up at the sky while they are speaking?

Motivating students involves many decisions regarding content, syllabus and methodology, but it can also be furthered or hindered by our managerial style. Eye contact is one such detail of teacher style that may have a surprisingly significant impact, especially in combination with the other techniques described in this chapter. Our support and encouragement of students who have a poor view of their ability in a large mixed ability group need not always necessarily be verbal.

Try looking at the class as you are speaking, allowing your gaze to travel gently so that you aren't staring inhibitingly at any one student. Do look at a student when they speak, but occasionally let your eyes rest on others as well (on the other side of the room) before coming back to the first one. (Experiment with the reverse process and see the – no doubt negative – effects of looking up at the ceiling, at the floor, or through the window as you are giving instructions or asking questions!)

'Our teacher just goes on and on'

A sure way of making students switch off is to speak in a monotone, regardless of what you are saying. Although proper voice training requires time and expertise, there are certain common-sense principles which all teachers may bear in mind as a starting-point for taking full advantage of one of the most valuable resources in a teacher's repertoire.

Change the volume and tone of your voice when the function of what you're saying changes, as this can aid the unsure learner, underlining meaning, intention and mood. It can also help to structure the lesson at a basic level. From my own experience of observing teachers, points in the lesson where there are significant voice changes include the following:

- beginning the lesson;
- stating the aims of the lesson;
- giving instructions;
- telling students to start a task;
- telling students how long they have to do a task;
- telling students how much time they have left to complete a task;
- interrupting students to point something important out;
- telling students that the time is up;
- asking the first and last of a series of comprehension questions;
- telling the class to copy something from the board;
- explaining a homework task;
- summarising what the lesson has been about.

The blackboard

In an age when the micro-computer presents such an exciting challenge to teachers everywhere, it may seem odd to sing the praises of the humble blackboard. It would, however, be a pity to neglect its potential in focusing the students' attention in class and in giving support to those who need it, in a simple and fundamental way. There are whole books written on the use of the board, so I will limit myself here to the following points, which I feel are relevant to keeping a class together.

- Use the board to record grammar, vocabulary and content, and point the students' attention to this information if ever the need arises.
- Use the board as a way of ensuring that your instructions are clear.
- Write up example sentences of the target structure on the board and remind students before the task (and during it, if they are having difficulty) that these are the structures they should be using.
- Use the board to jot down points made by the students in brainstorming sessions, as it provides a discreet way of emphasising the value of their contribution and of integrating it into the lesson where appropriate.
- At the end of the lesson, make sure students have copied any useful information from the board into their notebooks. Use what's on the board to remind them of the main points they have covered in the lesson.
- Implicit in the above is the fact that it would be wasteful to fill the board laboriously with useful information only to rub it clean again before you have given yourself time to exploit the material fully, and before the students have had time to absorb any of it.

Many of these strategies would strengthen the cohesion of any class, but for the student who feels lost or uncertain in a large mixed ability group, they become extremely important forms of guidance and support.

The most useful way to end this chapter is to offer the following teacher observation sheet as a practical aid to raising awareness of the more discreet aspects of teaching technique I have tried to describe. If you can, ask a colleague to watch one of your lessons, complete the checklist and discuss it with you; then you can do the same for them. If you prefer, fill in the observation sheet yourself after the lesson.

The Role of the Teacher: Observation Checklist

1 Was the lesson mostly about testing or teaching?
2 Did comprehension questions really check comprehension?
3 Did the teacher give reasonably accurate answers to the students' questions?
4 Was the teacher's reaction to the student's errors encouraging or discouraging?
5 Was the teacher sarcastic?
6 Did the teacher shout for no good reason?
7 Was the teacher friendly?
8 Was there any humour in the lesson?
9 Were the students relaxed?
10 Did the teacher use the students' names enough?
11 Did the teacher look at the students when speaking?
12 Did the teacher vary their position in the room according to the activity?
13 Did the teacher indicate how much time the students had to do an activity?
14 Did the teacher use the board to record useful information?
15 Did the teacher use checking techniques (questioning, elicitation) to focus the students' attention?
16 Did the teacher give students individual attention?
17 Did the students get the opportunity to use English to talk about topics that interested them?
18 Did the teacher adopt a different manner with different students? Did this have a favourable or a divisive effect?
19 Did the teacher's voice vary sufficiently to make the meaning clear and command the students' attention?
20 Did the teacher adopt different roles in the course of the lesson? What were these?

Further reading

Stevick, E. (1986) *Images and Options in the Language Classroom* (Cambridge University Press)
Underwood, M. (1987) *Effective Class Management* (Longman)
Willis, J. (1981) *Teaching English Through English* (Longman)

CHAPTER 5

Building on what they know

'Most students ignore most classrooms because most classrooms ignore most students.'

If weakness in the mixed ability class is the tip of an iceberg of potential strength, then what can the teacher do to tap the students' personal resources and improve their rate of success? What are the underlying causes of a student's apparent lack of motivation?

The fact that the English language and culture are unknown quantities for many students may make them seem ignorant or lacking in linguistic aptitude. Yet in their own language and culture, those same students are often voluble and witty. This is a truth universally acknowledged and yet rarely acted upon. The students' own language and culture provide a vast reservoir of material for the teacher, and a source of confidence for the learner. Nonetheless, they have been largely ignored by course designers and teachers, due to the influence of language-teaching theories that place a premium on the target language and culture. Students do not come into the classroom empty-handed or empty-minded; once we accept that learners bring with them a whole range of cultural experiences and first-language skills, then we can begin to build on what they know, instead of incessantly reminding them of what they do not know.

This chapter examines the practical applications of these latent skills in helping to bond mixed ability groups and stimulate a level of under-standing and personal engagement that will encourage students to overcome the different linguistic obstacles in their way. The suggestions I make here are all aimed at creating a rich, spacious pedagogy within which students of many abilities can feel confident and secure.

Cultural background, cultural foreground

In the past, English as a foreign language has generally been presented though imaginary situations based on the everyday life of a native-speaker family living in Britain or the USA. The people and events described were often banal and bore little relation to the students' own world. Nothing much of interest or importance seemed to happen to them, and therefore the educational content of language lessons seemed ultimately trivial.

However, the flourishing of English as an international language and the recognition of the links between the world of the language classroom and the 'real' world outside have brought about significant developments in methodology and materials design. The range of cultural reference to be drawn on has widened considerably and can be summarised by three basic types of context. The first of these is the native-speaker culture (usually referring to the British or North American cultures) which constitutes an important dimension to language teaching as, according to research, a knowledgeable but critical attitude to the target culture may promote learning. (See Svarnes, 1988.) Then there is the learners' own cultural experience (the ideas, beliefs, values and institutions of the society to which they belong). Finally, there is the international perspective and context, in which English operates significantly as a medium of communication. Its role here makes it an ideal educational vehicle for increasing the learners' understanding of a wide variety of other cultures, often very different from their own.

In a mixed ability class, it is vitally important to offer a 'way in' to the lesson by drawing on a broad range of relevant topics, rather than sticking religiously to what is covered by the course-book. When a class is given the opportunity to work around subjects that genuinely interest them, the teacher may achieve a dual purpose: those students who are struggling with aspects of the language will be encouraged to persist in their efforts because the content of the lesson appeals to them, while those students who are linguistically able will be more patient of a slow pace at times, because they are not intensely bored! It is for this reason of considerable value to ask your students what material they find most interesting and then work with that in mind. On one occasion, when I lost patience with a particularly tedious textbook (which included such topics as electric kettles, British car registration numbers and golf-balls), I decided to ask my students exactly this question. Here is a list of topics that proved to be popular with the groups of adolescent and young adult students that I asked.

- facts (science and technology);
- the English language;
- social problems;
- British culture;
- political problems;
- the culture of other countries;
- English and American literature;
- local culture;
- personal experience of students;
- American life and institutions;
- films;
- love and friendship;
- the future;
- sport;
- travel;
- television;
- beliefs;
- pop music;
- holidays;
- education.

> **Task:** Give your students a list of topics like these, or any others you find appropriate, and ask them to put the topics in order of preference or to give each one a score out of four for interest value (where 1 = uninteresting and 4 = extremely interesting).

The following exercises, covering between them local, native-speaker, comparative and international cultures, are intended as examples of how

to motivate a class of mixed linguistic ability by drawing on subjects that
the students can engage with personally and relate to their own cultural
milieu. The first exercise introduces the target culture in a light-hearted
and team-spirited manner, encouraging group cohesion. Activities 2 to
5 draw significantly on the mother culture as a resource; activities 6 to
8 explore different cultures on a comparative basis; and the final exercises
look at the world as a 'global village' or single community.

1 Great Britain quiz

Aim: to increase the students' awareness of life in Britain while practising
the Simple Present, modal verbs and conditionals.

1 Divide the class into two or more teams.
2 Hand round copies of questions like the following and allow five
   minutes for preparation of the answers. The questions should be of
   varied difficulty, and consultation amongst members of the same team
   should be encouraged.

True/False

1 In the UK, people drive on the left-hand side of the road.
2 If you go to Oxford, you will see Buckingham Palace.
3 If you go to London, you will be able to visit Shakespeare's
   birthplace.
4 You cannot use English pounds in Scotland.
5 You have to show your passport when you travel from
   England into Wales.
6 Edinburgh is known as the 'Athens of the north'.
7 If you go to Northern Ireland, you can visit Dublin.
8 The leader of the government in Britain is called the president.
9 There are 100 pence in a pound.
10 BBC stands for Britain's Broadcasting Company.
11 Prince Charles will be the next monarch of Great Britain.
12 The Conservative party are also known as Tories.

---

3 Allow the players to choose the questions they would like to answer
   when it's their turn.

Comments
Answers are as follows: 1 true; 2 false; 3 false; 4 false; 5 false;
6 false; 7 false; 8 false; 9 true; 10 false (British Broadcasting
Corporation); 11 true; 12 true.

By allowing consultation in stage 2 and a degree of choice in stage 3,
support can be provided for weaker students in this game. The group
effort is emphasised, and if variety is built into the questions, both in
terms of language and topics, individuals will have the opportunity to
participate at their own level.

Quizzes such as this can take many forms, but one simple modification
is to add 'wh-' questions of varying difficulty, as shown overleaf.

13 Who is Britain's most famous female writer of detective stories?
14 Which famous detective did Conan Doyle create?
15 Who was the British Prime Minister during the Second World War?
16 What is 'semi-detached'?
17 Who will be Britain's monarch after Elizabeth II?

2 Local shop names

Aim: to raise awareness of the way English is used in the students' own environment, as appropriate to individual interests and abilities.

1 Ask students to write down on a piece of paper the (English) name of a shop, pub or disco they know locally, or go past every day.
2 Circulate the pieces of paper and ask the class to identify the kind of place it might be. For example:
   'Highway' (disco) 'Culture' (shop) 'Galaxy' (pub).
3 Focus on one of the categories (for instance, shops) and make a list of the names on the board. Ask more specific questions. What kind of shop is it? What kind of people shop there? Is it expensive? Are the goods sold there locally-made or imported? Build up a chart similar to the following:

NAME	KIND OF SHOP	TYPE OF CUSTOMER	EXPENSIVE GOODS?	IMPORTED GOODS?
Culture	bookshop	students	no	both
Smart	boutique	women	yes	yes
Melody	music	teenagers	quite	both

etc.

4 Ask the students to suggest their own names for different kinds of shops, restaurants, discos, pubs, etc.
5 Discuss why English names are often preferred for particular kinds of shops.
6 As follow-up, ask the students to classify the names they have found according to whether they are nouns, verbs, adjectives or adverbs. Ask them to summarise the completed chart as written homework.

Comments
Similar activities may be based on supermarket products or the titles of books and magazines.

3 Local entertainment

Aim: to practise the language of entertainment; to personalise the topic and relate it to the students' own culture.

1 Give the students a questionnaire similar to the following one to complete in pairs.

Entertainment Questionnaire

Task: Answer the following questions. Score 3 for *often;* 2 for *sometimes;* 1 for *rarely;* 0 for *never.*

	YOU	PARTNER
1 Do you ever go to the opera?		
2 Do you ever go to the ballet?		
3 Do you ever go to discos?		
4 Do you ever go to the cinema?		
5 Do you ever go to the theatre?		
6 Do you ever go to rock concerts?		
7 Do you ever go to classical concerts?		
8 Do you ever go to pubs?		
9 Do you ever go to cafés?		
10 Do you ever go to restaurants?		

Now add up the scores for each kind of entertainment. Which is the most popular form of entertainment in your class?

---

2 Ask students to make a poster based on what's on in their town that week. Naturally, their sources will be local newspapers and magazines in their mother tongue; the poster will be in English.

4 Local small ads

Aim: to exploit the material from local English language newspapers in drama activities.

1 Ask students to identify the source of texts such as the following. (Where would they see them? Who would write them? Why? etc.)

Hairdresser wanted

Experienced hairdresser required for cruise ship. Tel: 418 0744

---

2 Ask students to prepare a telephone call expressing interest in the advertisement. They will need to ask for further information, and then arrange an interview. Provide a 'split-dialogue' worksheet, such as the one overleaf, to help them if need be.
3 The students then role-play the interviews, with several candidates applying for each job.
4 The class votes on who is the funniest or most suitable candidate.

Comments

Local English language newspapers give listings of television, cinema and theatre programmes, as well as business news, information on local restaurants and the weather forecast. Authentic texts may be chosen from amongst these according to the interests of the class or the requirements of an examination. The worksheet may be written up on the board or on an OHP.

5 Cultural cartoons

Aim: to encourage students to think creatively about the language they know in a motivated, non-competitive way.

1 Collect cartoons from magazines or newspapers and blank out the caption or dialogue in speech bubbles with Tipp-Ex, replacing them with an English equivalent.
2 Provide students with some cartoons that have been blanked out without a translation being inserted, and ask them to suggest captions or speech bubbles in English themselves.

Comments

Cartoons are motivating, but they are often culture-specific. For this reason, the style or subject focus of a local cartoon will often make it more accessible to the learner than one from the foreign language culture. The appealing cartoon form can thus be given heightened relevance.

6 Would you like to live abroad?

Aim: to make the students more aware of differences between their own country and the UK.

1 Ask the students what they would like about living abroad and what they wouldn't like. Build up a list like the following one from their suggestions. (Accept and translate mother-tongue suggestions from weaker students, as necessary – see pages 61 – 70 for guidance.)

```
 1 the food
 2 the weather
 3 the language
 4 not seeing my parents
 5 running out of money
 6 making new friends
 7 leaving my bedroom behind
 8 transport – nervousness about how to get around
 9 mixing with people from different nationalities
10 different customs e.g. ignorance about visiting routine
11 ?
12 ?
13 ?
14 ?
15 ?
```

2 Now ask students to copy these points into their notebooks, dividing them between two columns labelled 'like' and 'dislike'. They may add more items if they wish (11–15). A completed sheet might look something like this:

LIKE	DISLIKE
food	Different customs
Mixing with different nationalities	The money — worries about running out
Not seeing my parents	The weather
Transport	The language
Making new friends	Leaving my bedroom

3 Ask the students to compare their answers with a partner and report back on any differences of opinion. For example:
'George says he would like the food, but I know I wouldn't.'

4 As follow-up, ask the class to write a summary of the answers they gave, adding reasons where appropriate. For example:

SUMMARY: Living abroad

I would like to live abroad, but there would be some things I wouldn't like about it too. One thing I would like is eating different food; it gets very boring eating the same food day after day, year after year . . .

etc.

Comments

In Europe, travel abroad for pleasure, education or business is becoming increasingly common and easy. There are, however, many students who may never be able to visit other countries. By making the activity hypothetical *(would)*, this exercise allows everyone to take part regardless.

A variation on stage 2 is to ask the students to rank the items in order of importance for them.

Another version of this activity can be found in *Conversation* by Nolasco and Arthur (1987).

7 Ain't misbehaving

Aim: to make students more aware of differences in social behaviour between their culture and that of the UK.

1 Ask the class to get into pairs or groups and discuss how they would complete the following chart. Then ask them to consider how accurate the middle column on the UK is. Is there anything in it that they would want to change?

TOPIC	UNITED KINGDOM	MY COUNTRY
1 Invitations	More often invited to someone's home than to a restaurant. When visiting someone's home, it's customary to take flowers or a box of chocolates with you. When invited to a party, you often need to take a bottle of wine or even a pack of beer with you.	
2 Getting to know people	At an informal party, you don't have to wait to be introduced: introduce yourself. People usually stand at informal parties, and chat to a lot of people. People shake hands when they meet someone for the first time, but not every time they see them.	
3 Kissing	Men and women friends may kiss (on the cheek) if they have known each other for some time.	
4 Dinner	Dinner is usually between 6.30 and 7.30, though this varies.	
5 Time	People usually try to arrive at meetings and appointments on time, neither too early nor more than, say, 15 minutes late.	
6 Drinking	The pub is the most common place for informal meetings at lunchtime and in the evening.	
7 Buying drinks	A group of friends often take it in turns to buy drinks.	

| 8 Women in pubs | Both men and women go to pubs. It is fairly common for women to go to a pub without men. | |
| 9 Noise | People invited to dinner do not eat and drink noisily. | |

2 The students write what happens in these situations in their own country in the right-hand column. They may follow the phrasing of the sentences in the first column to write their statements.

Comments
This activity may be presented either as a handout, or if this is impractical, a blank chart can be drawn on the board or OHP and the teacher can fill this in by giving examples and eliciting suggestions from the students. If some students haven't completed their chart when the time is up, ask the pairs or groups to compare their answers in order to write in any information they still have missing.

8 Conflicting gestures

Aim: to increase the students' awareness of non-verbal means of communication and of the differences in use of gesture between the native and target cultures. For the weaker student, this may provide a new opportunity for understanding and self-expression, while everyone can enjoy the chance to experiment.

1 The teacher mimes gestures and the students have to guess what they mean in the British context. If you can, draw the gestures yourself or get someone to draw them for you. The following are some examples:

(a) 'I'm hoping for good luck.' (Index finger and middle finger crossed.) Point out the expression 'I'm keeping my fingers crossed.'
(b) 'OK.' (Thumb and index finger forming a circle – accompanied by a smile.)

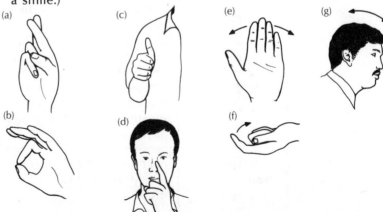

(c) 'OK.'/'Go ahead.'/'Well done.' (Thumb up.) Point out the expression 'thumbs up.'
(d) 'You're being too curious.'/'Mind your own business.' (Tap nose.) Point out the expression 'Don't be nosy.'
(e) 'Goodbye.' (Wave hand, palm outwards.)
(f) 'Come here.' (Index finger curled towards speaker.)
(g) 'Yes.' (Nod head.) Point out expression 'He/She nodded.'

2 Ask the students what, if anything, these gestures mean in their own country. Then ask them to complete the following chart.

GESTURE	GREAT BRITAIN	MY COUNTRY
(a)		
(b)		
(c)		
(d)		
(e)		
(f)		
(g)		

3 If one of the gestures is not used in their own country, ask the class to demonstrate what gesture is used instead.
4 The students then take it in turns to mime the gestures, or any others they know of (including gestures common in their own culture) and the rest of the class have to guess what they mean.

Comments
As a mixed ability variation, provide the students with a choice of answers for stage 1 in multiple-choice format. For example:

(a) 1 I'm angry. 2 I am hoping for good luck. 3 We are friends.
(b) 1 I have no money. 2 It was close. 3 OK.   etc.

Alternatively, give the students a list of 'meanings' to mime. They could use gestures appropriate to Britain or their own culture, and other pairs or groups can be asked to guess which meaning is being mimed, and whether it would be used in a British or local context. A list of such 'meanings' might include:

1 I'm hungry.	11 I'm afraid.
2 Excellent.	12 Sit down.
3 money	13 a long time ago/in the past
4 Goodbye.	14 Come here.
5 Hello.	15 Go away.
6 I love you.	16 I know./I understand.
7 Good luck.	17 He/she is very clever.
8 No, thank you.	18 What do you want?
9 yes	19 an insult
10 no	20 You're too curious.

21 It's a secret.
22 Be quiet.
23 Not so loud.

24 He/she is very good looking.
25 Can I have a word with you?

As follow-up, ask the students to prepare a mimed scene in groups, incorporating some of the gestures they have been practising. Some groups should set their scene in the local culture, others in a British context. Encourage a humorous approach.

9 Languages of the world

Aim: to help students put English in the context of other languages.

1 Divide the class into teams and play the following quiz.

> 1 Which language in the world is spoken by most people?
> 2 Which language has the largest vocabulary?
> 3 Which is the oldest written language?
> 4 Which sub-continent has the largest number of languages?
> 5 Which language has no irregular verbs?
> 6 Which language has the most letters in its alphabet?
> 7 In which language is the largest encyclopedia in the world written?

2 Give students the results of a survey of why people all over the world learn English and ask them to tick *their* reason for learning English and then to rank them in order of most common reasons why people in other countries learn English (given here in the correct order).

Why People Learn English	Ranking	My Reasons
1 They need it for their work.		
2 To talk to native-speakers for business/ educational reasons.		
3 To talk to non-native speakers for business/ educational purposes.		
4 It is needed in the society in which we live.		
5 A knowledge of another language will make me a better person.		
6 To get a better job.		
7 To talk to people who don't speak my language.		
8 I like countries where English is spoken.		
9 I like native speakers of English.		
10 I intend to travel to other countries for work.		

Comments
The idea for the quiz came from *Headway Upper-Intermediate* (Oxford University Press); the survey was derived from Willard Shaw, 1981.

An easier version of the quiz is to provide the students with the answers but in a jumbled order.

The correct answers are as follows: 1 China; 2 English; 3 Egyptian; 4 India; 5 Esperanto; 6 Cambodian; 7 Spanish.

10 Problems of the world

Aim: to encourage spoken fluency; to encourage students to use English in discussing international problems, to introduce contexts into the class that are not trivial.

1 Elicit from the students some problems of a global nature such as the following, and write them on the board.

```
        pollution    illiteracy    poverty    homelessness
        over-population    AIDS    drugs    terrorism
  the Middle East    survival of animal species    the ozone layer
   nuclear waste    nuclear weapons    local wars    starvation
```

2 Ask the class to rank these problems in order of their seriousness or urgency, and to give at least one reason for their choice in each case.
3 Ask students (in groups or pairs) to suggest solutions to the most important problems. They may, if they wish, simply match the problems with solutions provided for them by the teacher. For example:

```
 UN peace-keeping force    disarmament    send into outer space
     ban aerosol sprays    impose stricter fines    ban hunting
 find a homeland for the Palestinians    increase spending on schools
           return to family life    provide more jobs
```

4 The completed table can be used as a prompt for oral or written summary skills.

Through activities and exercises such as these, students can be allowed to learn from a secure base of the familiar. At the same time as being encouraged to perspectivise their world and to engage with new ideas, they will be expanding their linguistic capacity, refining their ability to express opinions, and increasing their overall confidence.

Making use of L1

Task: Circle the most appropriate answers in the following questionnaire, bearing in mind the problems of teaching a mixed ability class.

1 Should the teacher know the students' L1?	YES	NO
2 Should the teacher use the students' L1 in class?	SOMETIMES	NEVER
3 Should the students use their L1 in the classroom?	SOMETIMES	NEVER

If you said 'sometimes' in answer to question 2, complete the following.

Should the teacher use the L1 when:

4 explaining new words?	YES	NO
5 explaining grammar?	YES	NO
6 explaining differences between the rules of English and L1 grammar?	YES	NO
7 explaining differences between the way we use the rules of English and L1 to communicate?	YES	NO
8 giving instructions?	YES	NO

If you said 'sometimes' in answer to question 3, complete the following.

Should the students be allowed to use L1 to:

9 discuss pair- and group-work exercises?	YES	NO
10 ask, 'How do you say X in English?	YES	NO
11 translate a word into L1 to show understanding?	YES	NO
12 translate texts into L1 to show understanding?	YES	NO
13 translate as a general test of their proficiency in English?	YES	NO

Should the teacher and students use L1 to:

14 check listening comprehension?	YES	NO
15 check reading comprehension?	YES	NO
16 discuss the methods used in the classroom?	YES	NO

Now check your answers with those given by 300 students in a survey designed to identify their attitudes to the use of L1 in the classroom (page 164).

Attitudes towards the use of the mother tongue in the foreign language classroom have changed a great deal since the nineteenth century when the grammar/translation method was the dominant approach to language teaching. The direct method, with its emphasis on a more 'natural' process of foreign language learning that works parallel to the learning of the mother tongue, tried largely to do without L1 in the classroom, although it was still called on to formulate rules and gloss new words (see Howatt, 1984: 161–173). A more rigorous exclusion of the mother tongue came into effect, however, with the rise of the audio-lingual method in the fifties and sixties. Here, the theory of habit-formation in language learning made it difficult to see the use of the L1 as anything but a 'bad habit' which had to be broken. Yet even here, contrastive analysis was a deciding factor in syllabus design and the treatment of error, and this indicated a recognition of the implicit, albeit 'negative', importance of the L1.

In the modern communicative approach, the teacher's main objective is to get their students using language in ways which reflect the purposes to which it is put outside the classroom. There are no hard and fast rules concerning the use of L1 here; flexibility and the importance of realistic targets are two of the guiding principles behind the approach. Common sense suggests that students will learn more effectively if, for example, they have a clear understanding of the contexts in which the target language is used to communicate: the mother tongue may be useful in explaining these contexts, particularly at lower levels. The tasks students are asked to perform in a communicative classroom are often quite complex, and the English used for instructions in such situations can often be more difficult than the English required to complete the task itself! Again, the mother tongue may be useful in giving clear instructions or checking those given in English by asking for a quick translation back into L1. (The task itself should be within the reach of the whole class.)

It is, of course, important to remember that students can learn a lot from hearing instructions and explanations in English (even when these are slightly above their linguistic level); our main objective is also very much to expose them to as much comprehensible English as possible. However, there will be times when the use of L1 can provide support and security for the less confident learner, as well as acting as a launching-pad for communicative activities like the ones given below. The learner's mother tongue can be viewed as a source of strength rather than a skeleton in the cupboard, and its potential as an aid to both student and teacher alike should be maximised.

Most of the material in this chapter applies to lower levels and to those higher levels which contain an acute mixed ability element.

1 Eliciting English words

Asking for the English equivalent to a mother tongue word directly ('How do you say [L1] in English?') is often a quicker and less confusing way of eliciting language than the use of pictures or mime, for example. Students should also, of course, be encouraged to ask for English equivalents to mother tongue words in this way when they are writing or involved in a speaking exercise in class.

2 Explaining English words

An explanation given in the mother tongue can be useful either when the word is incidental to the main aim of an exercise or activity (and so a long-winded explanation in English would disrupt the flow of the lesson), or when there is a simple L1 equivalent adequate to the needs of that particular group or lesson. In cases where the teacher has planned to present the meaning of a new word in English, the weaker student will benefit from a quick check in L1 to make sure the word has been understood.

3 Contrastive vocabulary

Aim: to demonstrate the difference in the range of contexts and meanings that apparently similar words have in L1 and L2.

1 Choose a lexical area which raises problems because of L1 interference (for example, 'do' v 'make'). Give the class sentences to translate from L1 into L2. The sentences should contain the same L1 verb, where in English either one of two (or more) options would be possible. For example, the class could translate the mother tongue versions of:

> My father made a cake yesterday.
> I do my homework when I get home.
> I make my bed before I go to work.
> My brother does the washing-up.   etc.

2 Ask the students to devise a summary of the differences between apparently similar words in the two languages, in the form of a diagram or formula:

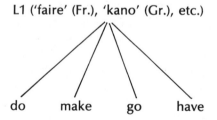

L1 ('faire' (Fr.), 'kano' (Gr.), etc.)

do   make   go   have

Comments
Such techniques work best in conjunction with others (giving examples, using pictures, inferring meaning, etc.), but they do provide a comprehensible summary that relates to knowledge the students already have.

4 'Know your friends' board game

The expression 'false friends' is applied to English words which look similar to mother tongue words but have a different meaning (for example, 'expérience' in French and 'experience' in English). These are also called false cognates. The term 'good friends' (cognates) refers to words that both look the same and have a similar meaning, for example, 'brother' and the German 'Bruder'. In a mixed ability class, both false and good friends provide culturally familiar territory for the 'weak' student, and should be exploited wherever possible.

The aim of this exercise is to make use of cognates and false cognates in expanding vocabulary and increasing linguistic confidence.

1 Write at least twenty-five words (both false and good friends) on separate cards. For example (for Greek):

sympathy, agony, philosophy, walkman, stereo, basket-ball, potato, radio, supermarket, garage, computer, semantic, typical, nervous, logical, pathos, culture, discotheque, tavern, pub, boutique, climate, automatic, telephone, thriller;

or (for German):

warehouse, brother, house, isolated, recipe, sensible, blame, serious, solid, actual, tablet, cultivated, protocol, spend, spare, consequence, sympathetic, eventual, chips.

Put the cards face down at the front of the room.
2 Draw the following grid on the blackboard or OHP:

Finish	F			F		F		←
F				F			F	←
→		F			F			
			F			F		←
→		F			F			F
			F				F	←
→		F			F			F
	F				F			←
Start	→			F			F	

3 Divide the class into two teams and give each a different coloured chalk or board pen. Members of each team take it in turns to throw the dice. When they land on an 'F', they take a card from the pile and have to make up an example sentence containing the word, to show whether it has the same or a different meaning in English and the mother tongue.
4 The first team to reach the finish wins.

Comments
This game can be played in smaller groups if the size of the class permits. In this case, the teacher will have to make copies of the board and word-cards.

The original idea for this game first appeared in *Modern English Teacher* (Vol. 9/2, 1981) in an article called 'Exploiting False Friends' by Patrick Woulfe.

5 Explaining the rules of grammar

The concepts which distinguish the Present Perfect, say, from the Simple Past, or which lie behind 'conditional' meaning, are difficult to put across at the best of times. With large mixed ability groups, where the students' speed and capacity to grasp new concepts and achieve proficiency in their practical application may be widely divergent, this area needs to be handled with particular thought and care. Diagrams and example sentences will of course be useful, but an additional (rather than exclusive) use of L1 will save time and should ensure impact and clarity of understanding with students. The explanation should be brief – it is not an opportunity to deliver a lecture on all that the teacher knows about English grammar!

There is, moreover, an enormous reservoir of intuitive (if not conscious) understanding of their first language that students bring to the English class. In attempting to clarify the importance of word order in English, for instance, or to convey the concepts behind difficult forms or structures, it will be economical to draw on this knowledge by comparing example sentences in the two languages. Students should be encouraged to summarise in a clear form, in a formula or a diagram if appropriate, the most common differences between the two languages. This will concretise certain rules or points of comparison for them, providing a clear and permanent guide for students to refer back to, as and when they need extra support.

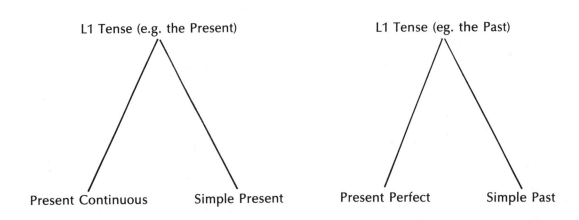

The mother tongue also becomes a useful resource for both teacher and student when the situations in which we use particular structures need to be explained. The English needed to explain the contexts of communication (role, attitude, setting, the shared experience of the speakers, etc.) is often more complex than the students' language level can cope with.

The emphasis in the following activities is on rules of *use* rather than rules of *grammar*. We understand more than we can produce in a foreign language (and in our first language, too, for that matter). This principle should enable us to offer the slow or shy student the opportunity to respond to a text in their own language (just as they might have to do in real life), rather than pressurising them into producing a response in

English. When the emphasis is on perception rather than production, it would be unfair to expect learners to respond by producing language exclusively in L2. The techniques described below allow the 'weaker' learner to perform in an area (the receptive skills) in which they may be relatively confident, without feeling that they have to compete in the more demanding area of written or spoken production.

6 *What did they say?*

Aim: to give students practice in paraphrasing the main points of a spoken message in their own language and to increase their awareness of communicative equivalences in L1 and L2.

1 Students form groups of three. Student 1 role-plays the part of someone who knows both languages, student 2 someone who knows only L1, and student 3 someone who only knows L2.

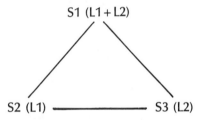

S1 and S2 are friends who share the same first language, while S3 is a visitor to their country who they happen to meet while on holiday. They discuss a topic agreed beforehand. The discussion, conducted in both L1 and L2, may be either free or based on role-cards such as the following:

Student 1
Ask student 3, who is a visitor from England, about their life in their own country; for example, their holidays, school, parents, brothers and sisters.
Translate into English any questions student 2 wants to ask student 3, and explain the answers in your own language. Student 2 doesn't speak English.

Student 2
You don't speak English. You want to ask student 3, who's a visitor from England, about life in their country; for example, how long their school holidays are; what their best subjects at school are; how much pocket money they get, and so on. Ask student 1 to translate your questions and student 3's answers for you.

> **Student 3**
> You're a visitor to a country where you don't speak the language. You meet two local people, one of whom speaks English. Tell them about yourself and your family.
> (You have two brothers and one sister; you have seven weeks' summer holiday; you get a lot of pocket money; your favourite subjects at school are maths and physics.)

2 Give the groups time to study their role-cards and prepare what they are going to say. The ensuing dialogue might begin as follows:

S1 (L2): Where are you from?
S3 (L2): From England.
S1 (L1): He says he's from England.
S2 (L1): Ask him if he likes it here.
S1 (L2): Do you like it here?
S3 (L2): Yes, it's very hot.
S1 (L1): He says it's very hot.

Comments
Other settings and roles for this activity might include 'At Customs' (S1 = bilingual passenger; S2 = businessperson who only speaks English; S3 = customs officer who only speaks L1) or 'At the Restaurant' (S1 = bilingual local; S2 = foreign visitor who only speaks English; S3 = waiter who only speaks L1).

An alternative to this activity which is much simpler in organisation terms is as follows.

Students are given a listening or reading passage. They are asked to explain the basic meaning of it to someone role-playing a character who doesn't speak English. For example:

● a news item on TV, on the radio or in a newspaper, to be paraphrased to parents;
● a set of instructions for using a piece of electrical equipment, to be explained to a neighbour;
● a letter from a penfriend, to a curious friend or parent;
● a song, to a friend.

7 Say it another way

Aim: to encourage students to use the English they know to paraphrase and simplify messages from their own language.

1 Whenever students ask, 'How do you say X in English?' or when they are at a loss for words because of a mother tongue expression they can't say in English, make a note of what caused the problem.
2 Draw up a list of these mother tongue phrases. Ask students to think of ways of expressing the same or a similar concept.
3 Finally, provide an idiomatic equivalent in English of what they originally wanted to say. The following is an example from Spanish (based on Atkinson, 1987).

SPANISH	SIMPLIFICATION	ORIGINAL MEANING
Es muy culto.	He's very polite.	He's very cultured.
Fue vergonzoso.	It was terrible.	It was disgraceful.
Se mostró reacio.	He didn't want to do it.	He appeared reluctant.
Le despidieron.	He lost his job.	He was sacked.

Comments
This activity could also be used in conjunction with others, such as 'What did they say?' or 'Community communication'.

8 Community communication

Aim: to encourage students' confidence in speaking, by allowing them to use L1 which the teacher helps them to reformulate into English.

1 Students sit in a circle, with the teacher sitting outside the circle.
2 The students decide what they want to talk about.
3 They talk, as much of the time as possible in English, and in L1 when they dry up. The teacher supplies an English translation when this happens and the student repeats what the teacher says.
4 The discussion continues until the students feel they have exhausted what they want to say on the subject.
5 The teacher provides them with feedback on useful expressions and problem areas.

Comments
The basic principle behind this area is drawn from 'Community Language Learning' (see Bolitho, *Practical English Teaching*, March 1983). The original version suggests that the discussion be recorded and played back, and also used later as a basis for further work. However, although there are obvious advantages in recording the discussion, it may be difficult to do this in classes where even arranging chairs in a circle is problematic. Perhaps portable cassette recorders could be supplied by the students themselves.

A more fundamental problem is that of getting less confident students to contribute to the discussion, without letting them get discouraged, or worse, excluded by the more outspoken members of the group. However, adaptations of the activity are possible. For instance, this typical mixed ability problem could be tackled by splitting the class into two or more smaller groups, with the teacher moving from group to group as appropriate, or by providing cue cards based on concepts, vocabulary and structures that would be useful when dealing with a text given as reading comprehension. For example, a discussion about the monarchy might require cards such as those shown on page 70.

Although there is some loss of student autonomy in these modified versions of the activity, they do to some degree overcome the obstacles that are common to large mixed ability classes.

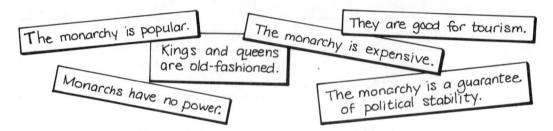

The monarchy is popular.

The monarchy is expensive.

They are good for tourism.

Kings and queens are old-fashioned.

Monarchs have no power.

The monarchy is a guarantee of political stability.

Conclusion

Perhaps one of the most common fears amongst mixed ability teachers is that they have in their class one or more students who feel at a loss or out of their depth – or who have simply failed to understand a new language item or instruction –, and yet who cannot communicate this to the teacher and thus gain help. It is all too easy for insecure students to feel isolated by incomprehension or their perceived failure, and to suffer a loss of self-esteem as a result. By adopting such strategies as those suggested in this chapter, the teacher can provide a framework of learning that is both familiar and confidence-building, and can thus tacitly remind learners of how much they already know, helping them to personalise their learning and take positive steps to acquire a new language of self-expression.

Further reading

Abbot, G. (1984) 'Should We Start Digging New Holes?' (*English Language Teaching Journal*, Vol. 38/2)

Adaskou, K. and D. Britten and Fahsi (1990) 'Design Decisions on the Cultural Content of a Secondary School Course for Morocco' (*English Language Teaching Journal*, Vol. 44/1)

Alptekin, C. and M. Alptekin (1984) 'The Question of Culture' (*English Language Teaching Journal*, Vol. 38/1)

Atkinson, D. (1987) 'The Mother Tongue in the Classroom: A Neglected Resource?' (*English Language Teaching Journal*, Vol. 41/4)

Bolitho, R. (1983) 'But Where's the Teacher?' (*Practical English Teaching*, Vol. 3/3)

Brown, G. (1990) 'Cultural Values: the Interpretation of Discourse' (*English Language Teaching Journal*, Vol. 44/1)

Duff, A. (1990) *Translation* (Oxford University Press)

Prodromou, L. (1988) 'English as Cultural Action' (*English Language Teaching Journal*, Vol. 42/2)

Prodromou, L. (1992) 'Cross-Cultural Factors in Language Learning' (*English Language Teaching Journal*, Vol. 46/1)

Svarnes, B. (1988) 'Attitudes and Cultural Distance in Second Language Acquisition' (*Applied Linguistics*, Vol. 9/4)

Tomlinson, B. (1987) 'Good Friends' (*Modern English Teacher*, Vol. 15/1)

Woulfe, P. (1981) 'Exploiting False Friends' (*Modern English Teacher*, Vol. 9/2)

CHAPTER 6

From closed to open-ended exercises

Task 1: How many of the following exercises and question types do you use with your classes? (A = *often*; B = *occasionally*; C = *never*.)

	A	B	C
1 Yes/no questions. *(Does Janet get up at seven o'clock?)*	☐	☐	☐
2 'Wh-' questions. *(What time does Janet get up?)*	☐	☐	☐
3 Either/or questions. *(Does Janet get up at seven or seven fifteen?)*	☐	☐	☐
4 Tag questions. *(Janet gets up at seven o'clock, doesn't she?)*	☐	☐	☐
5 Multiple choice questions. *(Janet gets up at (a) 7 a.m. (b) 7.15 a.m. (c) 7.30 a.m. (d) 7.45 a.m.)*	☐	☐	☐
6 True/false questions. *(Janet gets up at seven o'clock. True or false?)*	☐	☐	☐
7 Oral drilling.	☐	☐	☐
8 Producing correct sentences from a substitution table.	☐	☐	☐
9 Filling in gaps in a text (including cloze tests).	☐	☐	☐
10 Putting jumbled words in the correct order.	☐	☐	☐
11 Putting jumbled sentences in the correct order.	☐	☐	☐
12 Putting jumbled paragraphs in the correct order.	☐	☐	☐
13 Transforming sentences from one grammatical type to another (eg. active to passive; declarative to interrogative).	☐	☐	☐
14 Completing half-begun sentences *(Janet gets up . . .)*	☐	☐	☐

15 Connecting words and phrases by supplying conjunctions and other structure words (articles, pronouns, prepositions).

16 Replacing one word or words with another word or words (eg. replace 'he' with 'they' and make any other changes necessary).

17 Finding examples of a particular structure in a text (eg. underline all examples of the Present Perfect).

18 Finding examples of a particular function in a text (eg. circle all examples of 'apologies' in the dialogue).

19 Identifying the context of a listening or reading text (Who are the speakers? Where are they? What has just happened? etc.).

20 Matching (similar words, sentences, functions and grammatical forms, words and pictures, etc.).

21 Classifying vocabulary or information (eg. complete the following using words/information from the text.).

22 Completing a diagram using information from a text.

23 Labelling a diagram using information from a text.

24 Predicting the contents of a text (from a title, picture, words, etc.).

25 Comparing information in a text with visual information in a picture, chart, etc.

26 Spotting the differences (between texts or pictures).

27 Jigsaw reading/listening (students read/listen to different parts of a text and exchange information to complete the task).

28 Split dialogues (students use prompts to complete a spoken dialogue without knowing what their partner is going to say).

29 Students interviewing each other, completing questionnaires.

30 Describe and draw (student A describes a picture, student B draws it).

31 Dictation.

32 Describing a picture.
33 Using songs.
34 Role-play.

Task 2: Read this definition of open-ended exercises, then do the task that follows.

> 'An open-ended exercise can be defined as one that allows the learners to work in their own way, at their own pace, within the framework of one and the same lesson.'

Divide the exercise types in the questionnaire in Task 1 into those which seem 'open-ended' and those which seem 'closed'.

Many approaches to the problems of the mixed ability class, though useful, are difficult to implement. This may be because they take too long to prepare, or require equipment and premises that are simply not available. There is also, however, the difficulty that conventional responses to mixed ability problems, such as the provision of remedial exercises for weak students, may prove divisive and split the class into factions, as they involve the students working alone or in separate groups rather than as a unified whole. It is, in fact, not the existence of group-work as such that will help solve the problems of mixed ability classes, but what goes on *in* the groups. That is to say, group-work may help bring students of different abilities together to help and support each other, sharing diverse backgrounds and experience, or it may merely reinforce the differences in the class, functioning as a strategy for separating and keeping apart students of different linguistic abilities. Little will happen towards coming to grips with this problem unless the teacher is prepared to re-examine and extend his or her role and unless students are trained in such a way as to overcome any built-in prejudices towards different working methods and to improve their initiative and self-motivation (see chapters 2 and 3).

This chapter looks at the problem of the mixed ability group on the 'micro-level' of exercise types. It illustrates a particular kind of exercise, which involves minimal preparation by the teacher, while aiming to achieve the maximum involvement of learners at all levels within the class. The defining features of this type of exercise are:

- open-endedness, allowing all kinds of learners to work on the same task, in their own way and at their own pace;
- exploitation of the diversity within the class as an *aid* to learning rather than an obstacle to it;
- the perception of the class as a unified whole rather than as a collection of disparate parts.

I intend to draw on the exercise and task types listed in the questionnaire at the beginning of this chapter to help clarify the distinction between open and closed exercises, and I will attempt to show that even apparently 'closed' exercises can often be adapted and made more flexible. This argument will be developed further in the area of communicative methodology in the next chapter, to which this chapter could be said to serve as an introduction.

So-called 'closed' exercises

Many lessons are based on that well-tried formula 'text + questions' whereby a listening or reading text is presented, vocabulary items are more or less checked or explained, and the main business of the lesson is covered by comprehension questions which are typically of the kinds mentioned in numbers 1 – 6 of the questionnaire at the beginning of this chapter. In audio-lingual approaches to language teaching, for example, one of the teacher's main roles is to ask comprehension questions of this sort. Taken to excess, such an approach begins to resemble an interrogation or military exercise, while milder versions have often been compared to a well-rehearsed orchestra. Even at its best, the audio-lingual approach allows only quick and articulate students to build their confidence. The emphasis on choral work and the virtuoso solo performance, on thorough checking of structure, practice in oral manipulation and basic comprehension will really only benefit those students who can manage the pace, which is often fast and furious. Little allowance is made for differences in either learning style or proficiency level amongst students.

Although *Yes/No* and *'wh-' questions* are, in most cases (in theory, at least) not in themselves either open or closed, in practice they are often used as testing devices, even when teachers think that what they are doing is teaching. In this sense, such questions typically function as closed: they exclude the weak learner from full participation in the activity, and set up a hierarchy of good and bad learners, failures and successes. Faced with a closed question, the learner can respond either correctly or incorrectly. There is usually no in-between, and little room for manoeuvre or negotiation of meaning. The conscientious learner will probably get the answer right, and feel good about it; the weak or insecure learner may well get the answer wrong, and feel bad. This Manichean effect, a sifting of learners into sheep and goats, is arguably what we aim for when we are administering a test to the class, but it can hardly be argued, except perhaps by a member of the armed forces, that this approach is supportive and morale-boosting for weaker learners in the group.

Many of the exercises based on traditional question types place the student in a psychological corner, where anxiety is intensified and the fear of failure may lead to verbal paralysis.

'And when I am formulated, sprawling on a pin,
When I am pinned and wriggling on the wall
Then how should I begin?'

(T.S. Eliot, 'The Love Song of J. Alfred Prufrock')

What we should be aiming for, in contrast to this pedagogic claustro-phobia, is the kind of exercise which will allow the student to be at least *partly* right, to enable them to be constructive with their knowledge and develop their conscious strategies and intuition, rather than simply display their ignorance. Moreover, there *are* ways of making traditional comprehension questions more flexible, and more responsive to the needs of individual learners.

Look at the following 'wh-' question, for example:

What time does Janet get up?

At first glance, this question seems to elicit only one response: seven o'clock. However, when looked at more carefully, it can in fact be seen to elicit a wide range of potential answers:

seven
seven o'clock
at seven o'clock
She gets up at seven o'clock.
Janet gets up at seven.

In a traditional drill, the teacher (drill-master) may have insisted on only one of these answers as correct, because of the way that that particular drill was designed. Such straitjacketing is self-defeating, however, in a mixed ability group, and must give way to tolerance of a wider range of answers, both to stretch the quick student and provide achievable tasks for the slower one.

The question 'What happens when Janet gets up?' is grammatically similar to the first, but will, even at a superficial glance, seem to encourage a wider range of answers. It meets the needs of students who can or want to say only a little, while at the same time allowing more ambitious students room to move about. For example:

She has breakfast.
She goes to the kitchen and makes breakfast.
After she gets up, she makes breakfast and then goes for a run in the park.   etc.

The question 'What about your daily routine? Is it like Janet's?' combines both yes/no and 'wh-' type questions and may elicit anything from a monosyllabic answer to a short paragraph. It thus offers the kind of flexibility that should become second nature to a mixed ability teacher. (It should, incidentally, be routine practice to grade conventional compre-hension questions (re-ordering the way they are presented in the book, if need be) to allow for a smooth movement from easier to more difficult tasks. Fast workers can be asked to write more questions of their own while the rest of the class are finishing off the task.)

In the case of *gap-filling* and *cloze exercises* (where a cloze exercise is one which deletes words on a numerically regular basis – every seventh word, for example), a text can be made easier or more difficult simply by adjusting the number of words left out with a little deleting fluid and the use of photocopying facilities. The teacher then has two or more versions of the same text to distribute around the class according to the students' confidence and their view of their own abilities. Alternatively, the teacher can target specific word areas: John can work on prepositions, for example, if he finds them difficult, Helen on nouns and adjectives, and so on. Students who finish early can prepare gap-filling exercises for the rest of the class (or to do themselves as revision later on in the course!).

Students often find *multiple choice questions* something of a gamble: rather like a pedagogic version of Russian roulette! But much can be gained from approaching these exercises as learning devices rather than tests. The techniques for choosing answers should be taught in terms of a systematic process of elimination in which students apply their existing knowledge rationally and logically to new problems. Thus, they need to be trained to work out the principles which lie behind right or wrong answers, so that the hit-and-miss approach, so common amongst exam candidates preparing for multiple choice papers, can be systematised and invested with an understanding of linguistic principles. Grammar and vocabulary are two key areas in which awareness can usefully be raised. The significance of a verb formed with '-ing' or in the 'to' infinitive; choice of preposition or tense; collocations; stylistic appropriacy; cognitive meaning; these are recurring features in multiple choice options. For example:

1 Please _____ from smoking until the plane is airborne.
   (a) rest *(b)* refrain *(c)* resist *(d)* refuse

In the above question, *(b)* is correct, on grounds of meaning. In any case, only 'refrain' and 'rest' collocate with 'from', and 'rest' may be excluded on grounds of register, stylistic clumsiness and wrong meaning.

2 The committee chose me _____ the job.
   (a) do *(b)* to do *(c)* doing *(d)* does

In this question, *(b)* is the only grammatically correct answer. The sentence fits into a pattern of 'verb + object + 'to' infinitive', which may be contrasted with the syntax of sentences in which a modal verb is followed by a bare infinitive.

The important point here is to make the process one which involves more than just the skill of guessing correctly. In the case of students needing more support, deleting fluid can again be used to reduce the distracting number of options. Also, the whole class can be asked to try and fill in the answer *before* looking at the available possibilities; any answer they give that is correct can be accepted – whether it is the one provided by the textbook or not. If the multiple choice exercises are accompanied by a reading or listening text, students can be asked to predict the questions – and even the answers – before they see or hear the text. By using their linguistic and general knowledge and just plain common sense, the class as a whole, if not individuals alone, can often guess what meanings are probably concealed by apparently obscure language items. This is a process to which all students can contribute in various degrees. Rather than approaching multiple choice as a trap, set to catch them out, they should be taught to decode the text constructively, tackling it as individuals who have something to offer.

Drills and *substitution tables* work on the principle of the rapid production of a maximum number of correct sentences. They are hallmarks of the audio-lingual method, and although they may have a place in an eclectic methodology, one would expect them to be irredeemably teacher-centred. They can, nevertheless, be made more open-ended if we use them as the vehicles for involving learners. Specifically, one can use the board to construct a substitution table with the students' help.

Compare the alternatives below:

a)

Janet	gets up	at 11 o'clock.
She	has breakfast	at 7.30.
Janet's mother	goes to work	at 12.30.
John	goes to bed	at 9 o'clock.
He	has lunch	at 12.30.

etc.

b)

Students' names	Activities	Times
Maria	gets up	at ...

With the second (virtually blank) table drawn on the board as a starting-point, the teacher can elicit information from the class to go in the three columns (names, activities and times) and thus involve the learners from the very beginning of the lesson, at the same time personalising the task. The finished (elicited) version of the substitution table will reflect the abilities and interests of the class members and may look something like this:

Maria	gets up	at 8.00.
Yiannis	has breakfast	at 9.00.
Anna	goes to school	at 12.00.
Peter	wakes up	at 7.00.
Anthony	leaves the house	at 9.30.
Michael	gets to school	at 8.30.
She	catches the bus	at 7.30.
He	eats lunch	at 2.15.

When conducting the drill orally or using the table above as a cue for written accuracy practice, the teacher may apply a progressive fade-out technique, rubbing out cues from the board one by one, so as to make the task gradually more difficult.

Traditionally, *dictation* is a closed exercise: a text previously unseen by the students is dictated to the whole class in the same way, under the same constraints. If we consider what features characterise traditional dictation, we may see how to modify it in such a way that its rigid testing objective becomes a more flexible learning device, tailored to the needs of individuals with different skills and abilities.

Traditionally, dictation is:

- a fragment of text;
- drawn from literary sources;
- based on texts which are of little or no interest to the students;
- chosen by the teacher or the textbook;
- read by the teacher to all students together, in a ritualistic fashion;
- addressed to the students as isolated individuals working alone;
- marked by the teacher;
- scrutinised for errors;
- used to grade students into the good, the bad and the mediocre;
- a test of skills treated in isolation from other skills.

Here are some ways of making dictation less of a testing device and more of a mixed ability technique:

1 Ask your students to choose or contribute the texts on which the dictation is based.
2 Ask your students to choose the topics on which the dictation is based.
3 Elicit a topic from the students (eg. school, drugs, sport, etc.) and ask them to write down their opinions on it. Collect their papers in, and use these (corrected) student texts as the basis for the dictation.
4 Use varieties of English which may be more useful or interesting to your students, (eg. the lyrics of pop songs; the results of football matches, or other sports results; news items; railway or airport announcements; the top ten; a letter to a pen-friend, etc.)
5 Use complete texts rather than fragments.
6 Read the texts only once, at a natural pace appropriate to the type of text. The students write down as much as they can. (Tell them not to worry – they will get a chance to copy down the whole text later!) Then get them to work together in small, mixed ability groups to complete any gaps they still have in their versions by collaborating on their results. Go round the class and discreetly monitor their work, helping with spelling and difficult words where this is really necessary. By the end of the exercise, the whole class should have a complete and correct text.
7 Allow more fluent students to read the dictation occasionally. This can be followed by a second reading by the teacher for correctness.
8 Use the completed dictation as the starting-point for a discussion, or as the first part of a guided written composition.

The *true/false question* is similar to the multiple choice type, except that the choice of answers is more limited. Ideally, in a good test item, the answer is unambiguously one or other of the alternatives – either absolutely true or totally false. However, we said earlier that what often helps to build confidence in students is the idea that answers can be *partly* right or wrong. Thus, in the case of the mixed ability class, the virtue of a clear, indisputable answer key can be considered an obstacle to good teaching. Room for discrepancy can, however, be incorporated fairly easily into true/false questions with no extra preparation by the teacher. For instance, rather than ask students only to answer either 'true' or 'false', allow them to grade their answers according to how strongly they feel about them and their understanding of the text. Simply add a scale of 1–3 or 1–5 to the questions that are in the book, and instruct students to indicate their confidence in their answer by marking a number on the scale. For example:

> Fred felt everyone's eyes on him as soon as he walked into the office. He was on time, as always. The boss had noticed that, surely. Mr Bigsby didn't seem to like Fred, however. And neither did the others. He sensed their eyes on him, although they always turned away when he looked up. Yet he had nothing against them. He liked to get on with everyone; and he couldn't help liking them, in spite of everything. Perhaps he'd feel differently if he had married and had lots of children, filling the spaces, filling time.

UNTRUE ◀——————▶ TRUE

How true or false? – what do *you* think?	1	2	3	4	5
1 Fred is happy in his job.		✓			
2 Fred is unhappy in his job.					✓
3 Fred has a lot of children.	✓				
4 Nobody likes Fred.			✓		
5 Fred likes everyone.				✓	

When you write your own true/false questions, do not worry if you cannot make them water-tight, with definitely right or wrong answers. Ask students to rank them in order of importance for them, depending on how they interpret the text. Their answers will always provide a point of discussion and debate.

Naturally open-ended exercises: prediction

It is normal for teachers to work with the exercises that appear in their textbook or which have proved successful for them in the past. However, it is also important to broaden one's current repertoire, as it can be an uphill struggle working with a limited set of exercises in the face of the complex and unpredictable problems of a mixed ability class. Although the questionnaire that began this chapter only lists a few of the exercise types available to EFL teachers today, it does give them the chance to gauge the extent to which they are fulfilling their potential, and it will help to clarify the distinction between open-ended and closed activities.

The columns below summarise the two basic types of exercise under discussion:

CLOSED	OPEN
yes/no questions	prediction
'wh-' questions	matching
multiple choice	re-ordering
gap-filling	use of charts
dictation	labelling diagrams
drills	describe and draw

Although, as I have tried to show, the exercises in the left-hand column *can* be adapted to serve the needs of the mixed ability class, those in the 'open' category are more natural allies for the embattled mixed ability teacher. I would now like to consider three variations on prediction to illustrate the way in which this type of exercise can help the weaker members of a mixed ability class.

Students may be asked to make predictions in response to any number of different prompts: a picture, a title, the first sentence of a text, words from within a text, or just a topic written on the board. Predictions may be made on either the content or the language likely to occur in a text, or both of these.

While drills or conventional comprehension exercises run the risk of thwarting or oppressing the diffident or insecure student, prediction is pedagogically more spacious. First of all, there need not be one 'right' answer: all predictions are valid, though some may subsequently prove to be more consistent with the actual text. At the prediction stage, the learner is encouraged to draw on their knowledge and experience of the world and, where appropriate, their knowledge of other subjects, including school subjects. As discussed in chapter 2, a linguistically weak learner may be say, a computer buff or know something about farming methods, in which case his or her contribution is likely to be more forth-coming and substantial if the prediction is based on those subjects. The mundane daily routine of a Janet or John Smith living in Wimbledon or Camden Town is not necessarily going to help the weak student cross the threshold of linguistic reticence.

At all events, the process itself of prediction demystifies the text to some degree, and it will generally be perceived as more accessible than the same text dealt with through a rigid 'text + questions' approach.

1 Headlines and titles

A mixed ability approach to prediction from headlines and titles encourages students to draw on their knowledge of the language, their own experience, their knowledge of the world and of other subjects. This cannot happen if the subject matter of the headlines or titles means little or nothing to them. Look at the following examples:

A

| Is the new charter another watchdog that won't bite? |

B

| ROBOT MANAGER RUNS FACTORY |

Headline A is difficult to relate to any subject matter, let alone one in which the mixed ability class might be interested; it is also culture-specific. Consequently, only the linguistically able student will be able to respond to the teacher's attempt to elicit predictions about the ensuing article. In the second headline, the topic of the headline is explicit enough to elicit a contribution from more members of the class.

If a student, in an attempt to say something relevant to the subject, offers the wrong word but the right idea or, embarrassed, says the word in their mother tongue, then the teacher's response to this should be positive and encouraging. Indeed, such instances should be accepted by the teacher as useful opportunities to supply the right word in English. In this way, the student can be seen to be making a useful contribution to the lesson, rather than 'holding the class up'; a 'weakness' is transformed into an integral part of the lesson and made a strength.

2   Words, phrases, sentences

1   republic hundreds if chain excited hand
2   sauce mix salt heat fry
3   on the way, right on, put down, fifteen minutes, John Smith
4   take exercise, blood-flow, get up, drink milk, in the country
5   We are going round Marks and Spencers tomorrow.
6   Football hooliganism is becoming a serious problem in many
    countries today.

Write the above words and phrases up on the board and ask the class:
   'What do you think the text is going to be about?'
or:
   'Look at these expressions, and see if you can tell me some more words
   or phrases that you think might appear in the text.'
   While it is possible to make predictions about the kind of text suggested by all six sets of words and phrases, in a mixed ability class, 2, 4 and 6 will lend themselves more to student participation than 1, 3 and 5. The good student will be able to supply further words to go with those in all of the lists, but the weak student stands a better chance of having something to say in the lists with an obvious content. In 2, the possible subjects include cooking, recipes and eating (all pretty universal!) and in 4, most students will recognise the familiar and equally universal topic of health and keeping fit. Sentences 5 and 6 also illustrate the problem of culture-bound items, which make prediction difficult.

It is important to remember that we are not trying to 'catch the students out'. We want them to show what they know in a teaching, as opposed to testing, situation, not what they don't know.

3   Visuals

The kind of prediction exercise in which a 'weak' student can probably best excel is that based on pictures of different kinds, whether these be cartoons, photographs or textbook illustrations. A picture is universal and can cross boundaries in a way that words cannot. You do not have to be 'good at English' to guess what a picture is about, whether on its own or accompanying a text, and students will derive confidence from this fact. They can concentrate their effort on production rather than worrying about understanding the cues given to them. It is important, however, to remember to make the content of the material you choose stimulating both in itself and in terms of the interests of a particular class of students.

> **Task:** Consider which of the following pictures would stimulate your students to make predictions. What questions would you ask to encourage students to make predictions based on these pictures?

It is, of course, sometimes the case that the pictures one is faced with in prescribed course-books are of little interest to students and are apparently there just to make the text more understandable or to fill out a space on the page. In such cases, the best policy is probably to bring in, or ask the students to bring in, pictures of a greater interest and appropriateness (whether these come from books, personal albums, newspapers, or magazines). One can then either replace the course-book material entirely, or relate the new images to it as a point of comparison or simply an addition to the visual stimulus provided.

Finally, an important technique for helping learners to make the most of prediction exercises is to grade the order in which the various predictions are elicited. Here is an example for a possible order of difficulty (giving the easiest first):

- Topic on board, such as tennis, computers, clothes (can be chosen to suit needs of particular students);
- Picture (content interesting to students);
- Cartoon (without caption, preferably from the mother culture);
- Cartoon (with caption: language provides added difficulty);
- Sentence from text (grammatically complete, meaning explicit);
- Phrase(s) from text (grammatically incomplete, meaning less clear);
- Words from text (contextually related, easier to make connections);
- Words from text (randomly chosen, more difficult to predict content);
- Words from text, with irrelevant words thrown in as 'red herrings' (deliberately confusing and most difficult).

Open-ended exercises such as prediction, re-ordering and so on are not new, but have come to be associated with communicative methodology, which is the subject of the next chapter.

Further reading

Hemingway, P. (1986) 'Teaching a Mixed-Level Class' (*Practical English Teaching*, Vol. 7/1)

Prodromou L. (1983) 'Dictation: Pros, Cons, Procedures' (*Forum*, Vol XXI, No. 1)

Rinvolucri, M. (1986) 'Strategies for a Mixed Ability Group' (*Practical English Teaching*, Vol. 7/1)

CHAPTER 7

Communicative activities

Task: The table below lists ten ways in which communicative activities have been defined. Apply these criteria to the three exercises that follow by giving each one a score of 1 to 3 (where 1 = poor; 2 = good; 3 = very good). Then read the commentaries that follow.

Criteria

1 Language used for a purpose.
2 Focus on meaning rather than on form.
3 Learners presented with a choice of language.
4 Learners presented with a choice of meanings.
5 Language as interaction.
6 An element of unpredictability.
7 Authenticity of task – is real language used like this?
8 Authenticity of material – does it at least *look* like real material?
9 Is the material or task motivating? Does it make learners want to communicate?
10 Are the learners given the opportunity to express personal feelings, ideas or opinions through the exercises?

Exercise 1

Teacher: John has written a letter.
Learner: John wrote the letter yesterday.
Teacher: John has seen the film.
Learner: John saw the film yesterday.
Teacher: John has done his homework.
Learner: John did his homework yesterday.

Exercise 2

(Role-play in pairs)

CUE CARD FOR MS LOADSAMONEY

	YES/NO	WHEN
phone Bigshot		
write letter		
send letter		
find report		
copy report		

ROLE CARD 1

The boss, Ms Loadsamoney

Instructions:
Complete the chart by finding out which of the following your secretary has done and when.

CUE CARD FOR MR DOLITTLE

	YES/NO	WHEN
phone Bigshot	no	
write letter	yes	yesterday
send letter	yes	this morning
find report	yes	last week
copy report	no	

ROLE CARD 2

Secretary, Mr Dolittle

Instructions:
Tell your boss what you have done and when.

Exercise 3

Ask other people in the class the questions in the table below, and write their names and their answers in the appropriate column.

	NAME	YES/NO	WHEN
1 Have you written a letter recently?			
2 telephoned a friend?			
3 visited a friend?			
4 sent a postcard?			
5 sent a telegram?			
6 ?			
7 ?			
8 ?			

If you finish questions 1-5, think of some more questions of your own and ask them to the people in the class.

Commentary on Exercise 1

If we apply the criteria given at the beginning of the chapter to the trans-formation drill, we can see how artificial both the language and the task are, the sole purpose of the drill being to encourage formal accuracy in the production of the Simple Past. There is no choice for the learners either in what they say or in the way they say it. Their feelings, opinions, knowledge and experience are not taken into account, and as a result, they will not only have little wish to communicate during this exercise, but will be unable to do so even if they want to. Drills in their con-ventional form are not communicative, and their usefulness is limited in a mixed ability class. They may give students confidence in mani-pulating new structures – and this is important if any communication is later to take place – but the absence of choice, in language or content, makes the exercise a straitjacket in which 'strong' and 'weak' learners alike get squeezed. If students become restless (or worse, if the paper aeroplanes start to fly!), we should not be surprised.

Commentary on Exercise 2

The structures practised in this exercise are basically the same as those practised in the preceding one. For example, students would be expected to say something like:

Boss: Have you phoned Bigshot (yet)?
Secretary: No, I haven't.
Boss: Have you written that letter (yet)?
Secretary: Yes, I wrote it yesterday.   etc.

Although this mini role-play involves more of the features which help make exercises communicative, there is still much missing. It is more flexible than a conventional drill, but still too rigid for many mixed ability classes.

Commentary on Exercise 3

This exercise meets a lot of the requirements for a genuinely communica-tive activity. Although it still allows for some control, there is also an open-ended element to it. Thus, it should be possible for students of all abilities to find sufficient challenge in the task. The language is similar to that found in the previous two exercises, but moves from controlled practice to guided, to free practice. There is flexibility, too, in the students' way of working. If a student wishes only to speak with their neighbour, then the exercise allows for this, but more adventurous students can work with as many companions as are within earshot. There is also no need for them to finish all the questions; if the teacher wishes, students may be asked to exchange information, taking notes from each other and thus completing any blanks in their table.

It is important to stress that communicative activities are not in them-selves 'mixed ability sensitive'. Although they have advantages over the kind of drills exemplified above, they may still lack those qualities of open-endedness which characterise good mixed ability techniques. As we saw in exercise 3, an activity may be open-ended in three ways, allowing for:

- a choice of language (the Present Perfect and Simple Past, plus an optional 'free' element;
- a choice of content (topics either elicited from the students or of interest to them, with the possibility for early finishers of adding topics of their own);
- a choice of process, or of the method in which the task is to be completed (working individually, in pairs, trios, groups of four, etc., depending on the pace at which individuals work and on their preference for a particular learning style).

For the busy teacher, the possibility of using the same basic material with the whole class is most attractive: it eliminates the problem of finding and preparing extra material to supplement the needs of particular students. Whether taken from the textbook or devised by the teacher, the material should be exploited in such a way that the learners will be able to work as individuals while still remaining part of the group. Indeed, the lesson will be to a significant extent based on the fact that different students have different needs and interests. The lesson should actually gain from the diversity in the class, turning what is considered by many as a disadvantage into a positive advantage.

I will now go on to give some examples of exercises which have become popular within a communicative framework of language teaching. In each case, I will indicate ways in which they are, or can be made to be, more responsive to the needs of a mixed ability class.

Re-ordering

There are two types of re-ordering exercise I would like to deal with in this section: *jumbling* and *ranking*. While jumbling involves the students in understanding and manipulating a variety of linguistic devices such as linkers, ranking requires them to decide on an order according to their experience or opinion. As we shall see in the examples below, ranking is more open-ended than jumbling, but the teacher can introduce degrees of open-endedness to both types of exercise.

1 Free jumbling

Students are given a list of sentences and are asked to order them correctly. For example, they might be given the following:

It was a sunny day.
Suddenly, the third ant looked behind him.
They were on their way home.

> Three ants were walking up a hill.
> The question is, why then did the third ant say there was?
> In fact, there was no ant following them.
> 'There's another ant following us,' he said.

It is often the case with this kind of jumbling exercise that there is no one right answer. In this particular instance, for example, we could have both the following 'solutions':

Three ants were walking up a hill. It was a sunny day. They were on their way home. <div align="right">etc.</div>	Three ants were walking up a hill. They were on their way home. It was a sunny day. <div align="right">etc.</div>

The fact that there is more than one correct answer allows more students to be right than if there were only one correct answer.

2   Jumbling as text pre-construction

Before the students read or listen to a text, write the sentences randomly on the board one by one, checking their understanding of them. Ask the students to put the random events together to form a coherent story. They should compare their versions of the story with their books still closed. So far, the task has required the students not only to understand the sentences, but to use their experience and common sense to decide on a logical order. While some may excel in linguistic knowledge, others will be able to rely on common sense or relevant personal experience to make the task easier.

When the class come to read the text in the book, a lot of work will already have been done on the concepts involved, and the task of comprehension will therefore be less daunting, as the pre-construction phase allows the students a 'way in' to the text and its difficulties.

Comments

These re-ordering activities naturally work well with a mixture of individual work and pairwork. Students can be encouraged to complete a task to the best of their ability on their own, even if this means producing only a partially correct response. By asking them to compare their answers with a partner subsequently, looking for differences in their stories and completing any gaps they have left, you can ensure that less confident students receive discreet support while involved in exchanging stories and trying to solve a problem. The question of how many errors they have made in their answers should thus become a side-issue. In this way, a weakness – the inability to finish a task in the time given – is turned to good advantage, opening up the opportunity for students to interact.

It is vitally important to get your students used to the idea that you are not there to *test* them, but to encourage them to *use* language in order to fulfil tasks and solve problems.

Ranking exercises, like jumbling exercises, are not necessarily based on a text, although both can be used as a warm-up or follow-up activity. Essentially, ranking asks students to develop an opinion about the order in a list of items, based on their knowledge and experience. Whereas jumbling tends to work according to an external logic (of language or chronology, for example), ranking is more a matter of personal preferences and is therefore potentially more open.

3 Shipwreck

1 Tell the students they are about to be shipwrecked. Before their ship sinks, they have only enough time to gather a number of the following objects together. Which would they choose to take with them in the lifeboat?
2 They should number the items in order of preference.

aspirins	*sunglasses*	*clock*
sleeping bag	*warm clothes*	*raincoat*
pack of playing cards	*cheque book*	*the Bible or the Koran*
Chinese dictionary	*gun*	*Russian phrasebook*
camera	*notebook*	

4 On the move

1 Ask students to list all the different types of transport they can think of: *hovercraft, bicycle, ferry-boat, aeroplane, helicopter, car, van, lorry, motor-bike, moped, yacht, bus, tram, taxi,* etc.
2 Students then rank these in order of cost, comfort, snob-value and ecology.
3 Elicit from them as many possible solutions to the problem of traffic congestion in big cities, and write these on the board in random order. For example:
   ban all cars from the centre;
   build more car-parks;
   install more parking-meters;
   increase parking fines;
   build multi-storey car-parks;
   build underground car-parks;
   allow only residents' vehicles into the centre;
   allow only delivery vehicles access to shops;
   appoint more traffic police;
   allow parking on the pavement, etc.
4 Ask students to order these in terms of cost, practicality and effectiveness (for example).
5 Finish by asking students to use the ideas which have come up during the lesson as the basis for a discussion of the problem in groups or for a written composition as homework. The activities described here

will have provided guidance for less confident students, whether the
final task is oral or written.

5   *Crime and punishment*

1   Present students with a provocative or controversial crime, such as
    a mother who takes justice into her own hands and murders the
    husband who has been cruel to her for a number of years. (According
    to cultural circumstances, elaborate on the ways in which he was cruel
    to her and explain that it is after a particularly humiliating evening
    that she shoots and kill him.)
2   Ask students to work in groups to rank the following punishments
    in the order they feel would be most just:

       death sentence;
       life imprisonment;
       25 years in prison;
       charges dismissed;
       one year in prison;
       five years in prison;
       a short prison sentence and a fine;
       charges dismissed; recommendation of psychiatric treatment.

3   The students should give reasons for their decisions.

Comments
I first saw this technique in *Challenge to Think,* Rinvolucri et al.

6   *Literary texts*

A text may be tackled by asking students to rank statements referring
to it. The list of statements should allow for different interpretations of
the text. This example is based on a short poem by W. B. Yeats.

Politics

How can I, that girl standing there,
My attention fix
On Roman or on Russian
Or on Spanish politics?
Yet here's a travelled man that knows
What he talks about,
And there's a politician
That has read and thought,
And maybe what they say is true
Of war and war's alarms,
But O that I were young again
And held her in my arms!

---

1 Ask students to rank the following statements in order of importance depending on how they interpret the poem.

The speaker is an old man.
He is in love.
He was in love.
It is a time of war.
The speaker thinks politics are important.
He has travelled a lot.
The speaker likes to discuss world problems.
He admires politicians.

Questionnaires

1 Find someone who ...

This has become a very popular exercise in both communicative and humanistic language teaching. It is the kind of questionnaire which can be adapted very easily to suit the needs of a particular class. The grammar practised in it may involve either one or a variety of structures, and the teacher or students can choose topics they think relevant to their particular class. The following is an example of a standard 'find someone who' exercise.

a)

Find someone who...	Name
... wears size 40 shoes. ... plays tennis. ... doesn't like pop music. ... comes to school on foot. ... plays basketball. ... owns a bicycle.	

Compare this with the following mixed ability 'find someone who' exercise.

b)

Find someone who...	Name
... likes pop-music. ... comes to school by bus. ... saw the football match last night. ... went to the rock concert last week. ... has read a book in English recently. ... has worked in a shop.	

Comments

Both of these examples of 'find someone who' questionnaires have advantages over conventional exercises in a mixed ability class. The students can work at their own pace (they don't necessarily have to finish all the questions) and the topics are easily personalised to suit the interests of a particular group of students, thus helping motivation. Example 1, however, focuses on only one structure – the Simple Present – and is thus less flexible than example 2, which includes three different tenses, and therefore provides more scope for classes where differences in ability are greater.

Your instructions are vital in ensuring maximum effectiveness of exercises like these in a mixed ability class, as the following awareness-raising activity should demonstrate.

Task: Consider the following sets of instructions for a 'find someone who'. Which do you think are most appropriate for a mixed ability class?

(a) Ask other students in the class the questions in the chart, and write their name in the 'name' column. The first person to find someone who says 'yes' to each of the questions is the winner.
(b) Ask other students in the class the questions in the chart. If their answer is 'yes', write their name in the 'name' column. You must find a different name for each question.
(c) Ask other students in the class the questions in the chart. If their answer is 'yes', write their names in the 'name' column.

Comments

Instruction *(a)* encourages a competitive spirit in the students, which is fine if the teacher wants to make a game of the activity; but one disadvantage of such a game in a mixed ability class is that it might emphasise the differences between students and lead to a feeling of failure and frustration amongst 'slower' members of the class. This approach tends to reinforce the divisive 'winners and losers' mentality.

Instruction *(b)* encourages a maximum degree of interaction in the class. The greater element of luck in finding someone different for each of the questions also helps students to perform better than if the completion of the task were entirely dependent on asking questions quickly and correctly. However, in addition to taking longer to complete, this version of the exercise may be difficult to implement in a class where it is not easy for students to move around.

Instruction *(c)* allows students to work with as many or as few others as they wish, as long as they find enough names to fill in the chart. There is no competitive element. This is the simplest version of the activity, and probably the most suitable for a large mixed ability class.

Further suggestions for making this kind of exercise more flexible, and therefore more suitable for a mixed ability group are as follows:

● Make the questions more difficult as the questionnaire proceeds, by supplying short cues that need to be completed, rather than whole questions. This should present a greater challenge for faster students, and keep them busy while the others are catching up.

5 ... by bus. 6 ... 'Crime and Punishment'. 7 ... to the cinema tonight. 8 ... ice cream. 9 ... Spanish. 10 ... Bob Dylan record.	

● Leave the final question slots blank. Ask early finishers to write their own questions, which they can then ask other students.

7 ... the cinema last night. 8 ...plays the violin. 9 ..._____ 10 ..._____	

● In a later lesson, students can usefully be asked to construct their own questionnaires in groups, which they can then exchange with other groups to be filled in. This should ensure that the questions are on topics of interest to the students, as well as allowing students to find their own language level.

2 'Know yourself' questionnaires

The personal, 'human interest' content of these questionnaires makes them accessible to a very wide range of learners. Curiosity about themselves and each other should fuel their efforts to understand.

How Selfish Are You?

Answer the following questions by ticking boxes A, B or C, where A = *often*, B = *occasionally* and C = *never*.

	A	B	C
1 Do you ever ask others for help or advice?	☐	☐	☐
2 Do you ever show off your new clothes?	☐	☐	☐
3 Do you ever talk to other people about yourself?	☐	☐	☐
4 Do you ever criticise other people?	☐	☐	☐
5 Does it bother you when you don't get attention?	☐	☐	☐
6 Do you ever ignore other people?	☐	☐	☐
7 Do you blame others for your mistakes?	☐	☐	☐
8 Do you like flattery?	☐	☐	☐
9 Do you mind other people laughing at you?	☐	☐	☐
10 Do you like making fun of other people?	☐	☐	☐

11 Do you keep your good deeds a secret?

12 Does it bother you when you don't win in a game?

13 Do you refuse to admit you're wrong even when you know you are?

14 Do you mind other people using things that belong to you?

15 Do you find criticism easy to accept?

KEY

Give yourself 2 points if you answered *often* for questions 1, 9, 11, 15.

Give yourself 1 point for every question you answered with *occasionally*.

Give yourself 2 points if you answered *never* for questions 2, 3, 4, 5, 6, 7, 8, 10, 12, 13, 14.

Now add up your score.

- If you scored 20 or over, you are not at all selfish. However, people may take advantage of your good nature; perhaps you ought to stand up for yourself a little bit more.
- If you scored 14-19, this means you know when to stand up for yourself without being unfair to others. Congratulations!
- If you scored 5-13, you are pretty selfish, and you seem to quarrel with people all the time. Be careful, or you may soon have no friends left!
- If you scored less than 5, then you have very serious problems. You seem to think of no-one but yourself. Take a good look at yourself, and make some changes fast!

How Optimistic Are You?

Fill in the following questionnaire by answering 'yes' (✓) or 'no' (X) in the 'you' column. Then get into pairs and interview each other in order to fill in the 'partner' column.

YOU   PARTNER

1 Do you sing or whistle to yourself as you're working?

2 Do you feel nobody really understands you?

3 Do you make plans about the future?

4 Do you often feel bored?

5 Do you complain a lot, even about trivial things?

6 Are you easily disppointed?

7 Do you get enthusiastic easily?

8 Do you like your job (or your studies)?

9 Do you prefer spring to autumn?

10 Do you prefer black and white films to colour films?

11 Do you believe that 'time cures all'?

12 Do you try and amuse your friends?

13 _____

14 _____

15 _____

Now say whether you think you or your partner are optimistic. Why, or if not, why not?

Work with another pair and discuss and compare your answers. Who is the most optimistic person in the group? Why?

What other questions would you ask in order to find out if someone is an optimist or pessimist? Do you have any criticisms of the questions given? Which, if any, would you change, and why?

Comments

In this questionnaire, the learners simply answer 'yes' or 'no', and do not score points for the answers they give. The task is open-ended in the following ways:

● Learners have to discuss their answers in order to complete the task, first in pairs, then in fours. There is no cut-and-dried answer like a score to add up.
● Early finishers can think up their own questions and add them to the questionnaire. The class can voice their opinions on the questionnaire and modify it if they want to.
● If they choose to, any learner may work on their own, possibly never reaching the stage of interviewing their prospective partner. This is an important option in a mixed ability class, where students should never be forced to work with a partner or group before they are ready.

Open-ended pictures

1 Information-gap pictures

1 Get the class to divide into groups. Give a picture to some people from each group and tell them not to show it to the rest. The students who cannot see the picture now have to ask questions in order to gain enough information to be able to draw it.

2 The picture should be simple and uncluttered, depicting vocabulary items familiar to the students. For example, at elementary level, a simple line drawing like the following would be appropriate:

Comments

The task of asking questions and drawing the picture is probably more difficult than that of giving answers, but it is possible that a student who finds language learning difficult but who likes drawing would enjoy it and be good at it. Students should generally be given the choice of what they want to do, but it may be a good idea to try the activity in different ways: both in groups of roughly the same ability and in groups of mixed ability.

2 Describe and draw

1 The teacher describes a picture which the class has to draw.

2 The students compare their pictures and spot any differences between them. They then share their findings.
3 The class as a whole describes the picture using their versions of the drawing. Each contribution from the class is drawn up on the board by a volunteer, until the picture is complete.
4 The teacher asks how many students got the picture right originally. If difficulties or problems were encountered, these are aired and discussed.

Comments
This version of the well-known 'describe and draw' activity allows students to take an active part in the lesson, relying on their language or graphic skills, or a combination of both. The focus on accuracy in the drawing task diverts attention from linguistic accuracy, which, however, underpins the exercise. Weaker students should feel less self-conscious about practising, say, prepositions of place by this method than in a multiple choice test or gap-filling exercise.

3 Jigsaw describe and draw

In acutely mixed ability classes, you can use another version of the same activity. For this, you will need photocopying facilities.

1 Make two photocopies of the picture you intend to use (a black-and-white line drawing will obviously be best). Blank out certain details from each picture, but erase less from one than from the other.
2 Give each of the students one of the two versions. The one with a lot of detail missing can be given to more confident students and the other, more complete, version to students needing greater support.
3 Describe the picture and ask students to draw in any detail missing from their own copy.
4 The students then work in pairs to compare their final versions of the picture and complete them if they missed anything.

Comments
This 'jigsaw' approach allows the teacher to vary the level of difficulty of the exercise not only by erasing more or less information, but also by selecting particular language items to include or omit, according to the needs of individual students. Obviously, there is no limit to the number of different versions of the picture the teacher can create, and the greater the number there are, the more closely the activity can be tailored to suit the needs of individual students.

4 Draw, write, speak

1 The teacher writes a few items of vocabulary on the board.
   For example: *chair, table, vase, window, telephone, TV;*
   or: *tree, river, gate, hill, cows, farmer, sun, clouds.*
2 The students draw a picture to include any of the items in the two vocabulary lists, adding any other items they want to.
3 They then write a brief description of their picture.

4 In pairs, they describe their picture to their partner, who draws it as accurately as possible. They should avoid using their written description unless they really have to.

5 The students then write a brief description of the picture their partner has described.

6 They then compare pictures and identify any differences.

7 Finally, they compare their written descriptions and identify any differences in vocabulary, grammar or content. If in doubt, they can check with the teacher as to what is correct.

Comments

The vocabulary items in stage 1 provide guidance for students who have difficulty coming up with ideas for what to draw. The option is given to use or ignore these prompts.

The written description in stage 3 offers the opportunity to consider and consolidate linguistic knowledge, and, in the case of the more able student, to develop and extend this knowledge.

The option of consulting a written text while giving a spoken description of the picture provides students with support should they need it, without imposing it on those who do not.

Stage 7 should allow for peer correction and collaboration. In practice, more able students will be able to increase their partner's awareness of language errors, but the firm focus on content will provide a supportive framework within which to work.

Information transfer

Information presented in a visual form as a starting-point for practising the four skills is another hallmark of the communicative approach:

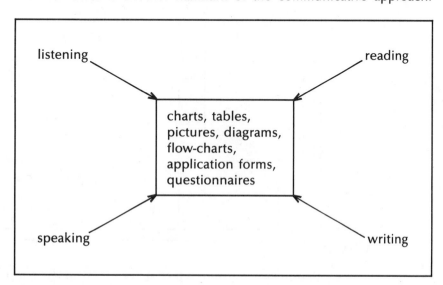

Thus, the class may be asked to look at an incomplete application form, listen to a dialogue and fill in the relevant information. They may then use the completed form as a prompt for interviewing each other. Finally, it may be used as the basis for a guided writing activity. In this way, all four skills are integrated, and one task leads naturally to the next. The following is an example using a map and a short text at an elementary level:

Read the text below and number, in the correct order, the places visited by Michelle, using the map.

Michelle is a French student living in Birmingham. Last Friday, she had a busy day; she had a lot of things to do in town, before picking her friend up at the railway station at twelve o'clock. First, she went to the post office and bought some stamps. Then she went to the bank to get some money. After this, she bought some tickets for the theatre, because her friend wanted to go and see 'Educating Rita', which was on at the Crescent ...

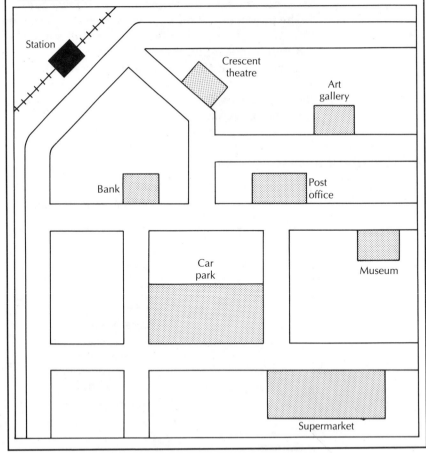

Information-transfer activities have a major part to play in the mixed ability class for the following reasons:

● Information in a visual form is comprehensible whether a student is linguistically gifted or not; visual information is a kind of 'universal language'.

● By integrating the four skills, information transfer techniques ensure that different learning styles are catered for.
● Charts and diagrams lend themselves to information-gap activities in which language is used for a communicative purpose.
● Information can be distributed in such a way that less confident students may receive more support in their task than more confident students.
● Students can often work together to complete a task, thus encouraging an open and sharing atmosphere among students of a mixture of talents and personalities.

A table such as the one below can be extended indefinitely along its vertical axis to make the task increasingly open-ended as regards the quantity and quality of language expected from the students. It can be extended indefinitely along its horizontal axis to accommodate the different speeds at which students work:

Have you ever...?	You	Partner 1	Partner 2	etc.
1 read *War and Peace?*				
2 seen a Stephen Spielberg film?				
3 been to Paris?				
4 ... *The Little Prince?*				
5 ... *Casablanca?*				
6 ... Budapest?				
7 (book)				
8 (film)				
9 (place)				
10 ?				
11 ?				
12 ?				
etc.				

Notice how the first column is graded to become increasingly more open and challenging: there is more student choice as the exercise proceeds, both as regards language and content. Some students may only reach question 3 (very controlled) or 6 (guided). Others will reach questions 10–12 and be able to choose both what to say and how to say it. Students will have the opportunity to fill in any blanks they have in their chart, both at the checking phase when the class reports back on their results and in the information-exchange phase, when they get into pairs or small groups to tell each other what they have discovered. In short, information-transfer exercises allow students to find their own level while working on the same task. Preparation time is minimal, and oral and written practice are amply provided for.

This chapter has looked at some of the typical exercises found in recent textbooks, especially those designed along communicative lines. It may be necessary for the mixed ability teacher to adapt some of these exercises in order to make them more open-ended and appropriate for the wide range of aptitude in a mixed ability class. There are, of course, many more exercises of the type discussed and illustrated in this chapter which may be followed up in the bibliography. My purpose has been to establish the basic principles behind open-ended communicative activities.

Further reading

Candlin, C. (ed.) (1981) *The Communicative Teaching of English* (Longman)

Nolasco, R. and L. Arthur (1987) *Conversation* (Oxford University Press)

Norman, D., U. Levihn and J. Hedenquist (1986) *Communicative Ideas* (Language Teaching Publications)

Revell, J. (1979) *Teaching Techniques for Communicative English* (Macmillan)

Rinvolucri, M. and J. Morgan (1988) *The Q Book* (Longman)

CHAPTER 8 | Drama techniques

'There is no magic formula for dealing with difficult students – the silent or the over-talkative. Do not forget, however, that learning depends on the students' feeling of well-being and self-esteem.
(Maley and Duff, 1982)

Earlier, I discussed two principles that can help to solve some of the problems of the mixed ability class: that of language learning in the context of related cultural factors, and that of open-ended exercises, which allow learners of all types to work at their own pace and in their own style within the framework of the same lesson.

Drama techniques combine both of these principles in potentially the most complete and effective manner. Although the very term 'drama' is difficult to define, I shall take it to refer to techniques which draw on and develop the emotional and cognitive capacities of the individual in activities which appeal to imagination and powers of self-expression. They include fairly obviously 'theatrical' activities such as mime, role-play and the performance of sketches; but they also include activities based on voice, movement and body language. There is often a strong element of unpredictability in drama, which teachers may exploit in improvisation activities and drama games.

'Drama is like the naughty child who climbs the high walls and ignores the No Trespassing sign. Drama may involve music, history, painting, mathematics, ski-ing, photography, cooking – anything. It does not respect subject barriers.'
(ibid.)

The techniques in this chapter attempt, in varying degrees, to fulfil the following conditions:

- They involve the students' personalities and ideas.
- They are open-ended.
- They encourage students to take risks, while recognising that shy students have the right to remain silent or withdrawn.
- They recognise the importance of self-esteem in all learners.
- They recognise that students have bodies as well as brains and that sitting still for long periods is bad for one's mental and physical well-being.
- They assert that failure has no place in the mixed ability class.
- They try to make students both self-aware and aware of others.
- The teacher's role is crucial, and though it varies widely, it is generally not at the centre of the classroom stage.

You will find that some of the techniques are familiar tools in a drama teacher's repertoire, some are original; but all of them have been adapted to suit the needs of the mixed ability class as defined in this book. Many traditional drama activities, challenging though they are, risk overwhelming the shy or linguistically insecure student. I have introduced a greater degree of guidance, structure and flexibility than may normally be found in this kind of exercise.

Breaking the ice

This section suggests quick ways of getting a new class of students to relax and feel less self-conscious.

1 Look down, look up, look round

1 Ask the students to stand up and look first at their feet for one minute, then up at the ceiling for another minute.
2 Ask them to find a partner and stand back to back for one minute.
3 Ask them to turn round and look at their partner in the eyes, keeping a straight face. Anyone who laughs is 'out'. The last pair to laugh are the winners.

Comments
I first learnt this idea from Charlyn Wessels (see bibliography).

2 Circular introductions

1 The first student says, 'My name is [Luke] and I like music.'
2 The second student repeats, 'His name is [Luke] and he likes music,' and continues, 'My name is [Maria] and I like football.'
3 The third student repeats what both the previous students have said and adds his or her own introduction. This continues around the group until everyone has introduced themselves.

Comments
Ideally, students should form small circles of about six or seven for this, but it will work in large, cramped classes with students staying where they are.

The repetition involved becomes a source of amusement as the activity progresses, and at the same time offers guidance for less confident students.

The activity can also be done as 'speak and mime': students accompany their 'likes' (music, football, swimming, etc.) with a mimed action, which has to be repeated by the next student in turn.

3 If ... do

1 The teacher makes statements and describes actions which the students must follow only if the statements are true of themselves. For example:
　'If your name is John, look up.'
　'If you have blue eyes, touch your toes.'

The statements can use simple or more complex language depending on the ability of the class:

If you are tall ...
If you have brown eyes ...
If you live near this school ...
If you are wearing something green ...
If you are left-handed ...
If you like ice-cream ...

The accompanying instruction can also be expressed in language of varying complexity.

... look up.
... look down.
... raise your arms.
... raise your left arm.
... look down at your feet.
... touch your nose.
... close your left eye.
... take your neighbour's pen and put it behind your ear.

2 Stop the activity at unexpected moments to check whether the students have indeed understood sufficiently well to respond to the statements which apply to them.

Comments
This is a variation on the traditional children's game, 'Simple Simon Says', and draws on the principles behind Total Physical Response, one of the so-called 'humanistic' approaches to language learning. One advantage of the activity (and the method) in mixed ability classes is that the students are not obliged to say anything. The language level can also easily be tailored by the teacher to meet the needs of the class.

4 Getting-to-know-you questionnaires

1 The teacher prepares a worksheet that contains a simple question-naire, designed to elicit information from a new class of language students.

QUESTIONNAIRE	
Name _____ Surname ____	Name _____ Surname ____
Address _____	Address _____
Tel. _____	Tel. _____
Favourite colour _____	Favourite colour _____
Hobbies _____	Hobbies _____

Name _____ Surname ____	Name _____ Surname ____
Address _____	Address _____
Tel. _____	Tel. _____
Favourite colour _____	Favourite colour _____
Hobbies _____	Hobbies _____
Name _____ Surname ____	Name _____ Surname ____
Address _____	Address _____
Tel. _____	Tel. _____
Favourite colour _____	Favourite colour _____
Hobbies _____	Hobbies _____

2 The students interview each other, completing as many sets of questions as their speed and ability permits.
3 The students introduce the people they have interviewed to the rest of the class, using their completed questionnaires.

Comments
As with many of the exercises in this section, this activity can be done as a 'walking around the room activity', if circumstances permit. Alternatively, the students can remain in their seats and interview the people sitting in front of them, behind them and to either side of them. Weak students not only have the option of completing fewer questions than faster members of the class, but also of using simpler language. Thus, while confident students should be encouraged to practise the questions in full, others may prefer simply to read out the words on the page; the very diffident may even remain silent while their partner gives them information to jot down.

Getting to know each other better

The following exercises are more appropriate for later on in a language course, when the students have grown more familiar and confident with each other.

1 Share and share alike

1 The teacher asks the students to write down information based on between two and four topics from a list such as the following:

My favourite TV programme _____
My favourite school subject _____
The (famous) person I most dislike _____
My favourite day of the week _____
The film I would least like to see at the cinema this week _____

2   The students go round the class (or consult those sitting nearest to them) to find the people who have at least one answer in common with their own.

Comments
The choice in stage 1, and the relatively easy task of finding at least one item in common with someone else, gives everyone in the class the opportunity to write as much as they want, and to speak to many or just a few students, according to their speed and ability.

2   Memories are made of words

1   The teacher writes the following expressions on the board:

Food's ready!   Time for bed!   It's getting dark.   Come in now!
Switch the light off and go to sleep.   You've got school tomorrow.
Just look at your clothes!   Can you two stop fighting?

---

2   The teacher elicits from the students or explains to them where these expressions might be heard (*parents speaking to their children*). The teacher asks the students to copy down only those phrases that their parents used to say to them when they were young, then to add any more they can think of themselves, if they wish. Mother-tongue expressions should, with the teacher's help, be translated into English.
3   The completed sheets of paper are then collected in, jumbled up and circulated round the class. The students write their name next to those expressions that their parents used to use, before passing the sheet on to another student.
4   The teacher 'freezes' the activity, and the students read out what is on the piece of paper they are holding at that point. They report which students share similar memories, by reading the names written on the paper at that stage. For example:
    'And don't stay out too late. John, Maria, Peter, Lena.'
5   As follow-up, ask the students why they think their parents said the things they did and how they themselves reacted.
6   The students write a dialogue in class or for homework, including as many of the expressions, or memories, as they can.

Comments
The number of example sentences the teacher gives at the beginning depends on how much guidance the class as a whole needs, in particular its less confident members. Although a class may only be as good as the weakest student, a balance must be kept between freedom and guidance to avoid frustrating either 'faster' or 'slower' learners.
    It is important to accept suggestions in the mother tongue to allow less confident students greater participation in the activity.

3   Photographic memory

1   The teacher asks the students to find a photograph from the family album or a magazine and to bring it to class. (The teacher should have

a collection of magazine photographs in reserve for the students who fail to do this!)

2 Working in pairs, and using dictionaries if they wish, the students write a brief description of the photograph they have chosen. They can write this in note-form if they like, or just make a list of points on what the photograph contains.

3 The teacher collects the descriptions in with their respective photographs.

4 The students then try and remember as much as they can about their picture, in order to describe it again as accurately as possible in writing.

5 The teacher collects in the new descriptions and puts them together with the original ones and the photographs that prompted them. These are then given to another pair of students to check. They compare all the pieces against one another, and 'correct' the description written from memory by writing in any missing details.

6 The pairs report back on how many errors of memory (not language) the other pairs made.

Comments

As this is a memory game, the students should be allowed to jot down their ideas either in note-form or full sentences, depending on their own particular level. One student may be good at English but have a bad memory, whereas another, who is struggling with English, may have a photographic memory!

Getting up and doing it

Having broken down inhibitions with such activities as 1–7, your students may be ready for more adventurous work, as described below. These activities encourage them to use their thinking, feeling and doing capacities to a greater extent than in conventional classroom activities, and thus aim to increase their confidence and encourage in the whole class a more co-operative and supportive role in the learning process.

1 Mixed mime

1 The teacher divides the class into groups, composed of mixtures of different learning types. Each group chooses a job and an action to mime. The action should be typical of the job chosen. For example:

> *Teacher: pointing to student;*
> *writing on board;*
> *marking homework.*

2 This information is written on pieces of paper, which the teacher collects in and mixes up.

3 The teacher then puts them on a table at the front of the class, face down, and invites students to come out to the front in pairs to draw

a slip of paper and perform the actions while the other groups guess what the job might be.

Comments

Stage 1 allows less confident learners to benefit from the support of other members of the group, and to fall back on the mother tongue if necessary. Stage 2 ensures that whatever is said in the mixed groups is translated into English by one of them. In stage 3, the mimed actions are based on information written by the students themselves, so, just as linguistic support has been provided in the group-work phase, here the students provide each other with imaginative support.

Asking students to come to the front and perform on their own should be avoided. The teacher should perhaps invite a couple of confident or extrovert students to begin with, before going on to a more mixed pair.

2 Concertina consequences

Aim: to practise writing skills.

1 The teacher reads the students a story, or, alternatively, the students read one themselves (a textbook narative will do).
2 The teacher asks them to form groups of six to eight and to sit round in circles.
3 The teacher explains that they should write a summary of the story on a sheet of paper (not in their notebooks) using typical narrative structures and linking devices; for example, the Simple Past, the Past Continuous, the Past Perfect; connectors such as 'first', 'next', 'suddenly', 'at last'; etc.
4 The students each write the first sentence on their sheet of paper. It can be short or long, simple or complex. They have three minutes to do this.
5 The teacher tells them to stop and fold their sheets over to conceal what they have written. It doesn't matter if they haven't finished. They just pass their sentence on to the person sitting next to them.
6 The teacher asks everyone to write the next sentence of their story on the sheet of paper that has just been handed to them. They have two to three minutes to do so.
7 The teacher asks them to stop again. The procedure repeats itself, as in stage 5, until the sheet of paper has returned to its original owner.
8 The students then take it in turns to read out their stories.

Comments

This technique allows students of all abilities to work at their own level, while collaborating on a writing task. If the class has acute mixed ability problems, the instructions in stage 4 can be changed to allow even greater flexibility (the 'concertina' effect). For example, they could be told to write a word, phrase or sentence. However little a student writes or however incorrect the writing is, folding over the sheet of paper will reduce their embarrassment. Homework would then be to write out the story in full, concentrating on making it flow and trying to eliminate errors. When the students hand in their homework, any outstanding errors can be dealt with on the board or on the OHP, ensuring that anonymity of error is preserved so that students do not feel in any way threatened or humiliated.

3 Oral concertina

Aim: to practise speaking skills.

1 The teacher tells the students a story or the students read one themselves in the textbook they are using.
2 The teacher, or one of the more fluent students, starts to re-tell the story. One sentence is enough.
3 The next student (chosen at random by the teacher) continues the story with as little as a word or as much as a sentence. Even if they say only one word, the student that follows must continue from where the previous speaker has stopped.
4 When the story has been reconstructed orally in the manner described above, the students should write a summary either in groups or for homework.

Comments

It is a good idea to warn the class that they will be expected to write a summary when the oral story-telling is over; this will encourage them to listen carefully to each other speaking. Obviously, the smaller the group, the more involvement is achieved. It may therefore be preferable to do one story with the whole class as an example first and then split them up into groups.

If you don't have a suitable story to use, or if you want to encourage your students to use their imaginations, just give the class a title to get them going.

If the class is particularly mixed, ask the students to write down a couple of ideas before you begin the oral reconstruction. Doing this will not only give them a greater sense of security, but will also ensure a steady flow of suggestions as the story unfolds around the class.

4 From face-to-face to back-to-back

Aim: to practise the Present Continuous and the language of description.

1 Students stand up and face each other in pairs.
2 They look very carefully at what their partner is wearing. (This is for two minutes.)
3 They sit down and write sentences in the Present Continuous, describing what their partner is wearing.
4 The teacher collects in what they have written and reads out some of the descriptions (correcting errors without comment). The students are asked to identify who is being described.
5 The teacher then asks half the class to come to the front.
6 The teacher distributes the written descriptions amongst the rest

of the class, who have to match these with the students at the front.
As students are identified, they go and sit down again.

7 The last student to be identified stays at the front and turns their back
   while the rest describe another member of the class to them. The
   student at the front has to guess who the person being described is.

8 Now the students go back into their original pairs and take it in turns
   to stand back-to-back in front of the class and describe what their
   partner is wearing. The rest of the class listen and report back at the
   end, correcting any lapses of memory, but not language errors. For
   example:
   'Maria said John is wearing a blue shirt, but he's wearing a red one.'

Comments

The transition from face-to-face to back-to-back is a movement from more
controlled to freer activity that allows everyone to participate, while not
cramping the more proficient. The writing in stage 3 allows 'weaker'
students to benefit from the teacher's help, and will provide support
for speaking in stages 6 and 8.

According to your students' ability, you could either allow them to
describe their original partner in stage 8, or give them a different partner
to increase the challenge. If necessary, allow students to consult their
original notes when performing the back-to-back; do, however,
discourage them from just reading out what they have written.

5 Games pupils play

Aim: to practise reading and writing skills through mime activities.

1 The students sit in groups of four. Give each group the rules of various
   games involving physical activity. (These should not be well-known
   games like football or basketball. Five examples follow.)

2 Each group studies the rules of their game and then decides how they
   are going to mime it to the other groups. They are not allowed to
   use actual objects or 'props'; these must also be mimed. One student
   in each group will act as the referee; the others will be the players
   or contestants.

3 As each group presents its game (following the written rules strictly),
   the other groups write down what they think the rules are.

4 When each group has done its mime, the class should be given time
   to finish writing down the rules of what they have seen.

5 When the rules have been reconstructed as accurately as possible
   by each group, the class can compare them with each other and with
   the original rules given to the groups.

A *Sack Race*

1 Two teams. The first contestant in each team stands at the starting-line in a sack, which should reach up to the contestant's waist.
2 The referee starts the game (by blowing a whistle or saying, 'On your marks. Get set. Go!')
3 One member from each team jumps to the other end of the room in the sack, touches the wall, and jumps back again.
4 When the first member of the team has returned to the starting-line, the second gets into the sack and continues the race. This continues until everyone in the team has taken part. (This may be as few as two.)
5 The first team to have all its members back at the starting-line wins.

C *Burst the Balloon Race*

1 Two teams, each of which should have at least two members. Everyone has a large balloon (large enough to sit on!).
2 When the referee starts the game, the first player in each team runs to the other end of the room, touches the wall, then sits on their balloon and bursts it.
3 When the first player has burst their balloon, they run back to the starting-line, and the next player in the team sets off.
4 The game finishes when all the members of a team have burst their balloons in this way and are back at the starting-post.

B *Egg and Spoon Race*

1 Two teams. Each team (which may, on occasions, consist of only one person) has a soup spoon with an egg (or potato) in it.
2 When the referee starts the race, the first member of each team runs to the other end of the room, touches the wall, and runs back to the starting-line.
3 The second member of the team takes the spoon and continues the race.
4 The game only ends when all the members of a team have run to the opposite wall and back again. The first team to do this without dropping the egg (or potato) wins.

D *Don't Spill the Water Race*

1 Two teams, with at least two members each. Both teams have a small tray or saucer with a plastic beaker full of water on it.
2 When the referee gives the signal to start, the first member of each team runs with the tray and beaker to the other end of the room, trying to spill as little water as possible. They must not touch the beaker as they run.
3 When the first runner gets back to the starting-line, they hand the tray and water to the next member of the team, who runs with it to the other end of the room, spilling as little of the water as possible.
4 The winning team not only has to get all its members back to the finishing-line first, but must have spilt less water than any other team.
5 The referee must check the quantity of water in each beaker.

E *Grab and run*

1 Two teams, with at least two students in each.
2 The two teams stand at least two metres away from a circle one metre in diameter. A ball (or any other object like a rag or plastic cup) is placed in the middle.
3 A member from each team stands in the circle; they face each other.
4 When the referee gives the signal to start the game, each player in the circle tries to grab the ball and run back to their team without being 'caught' by the opposing player. To catch an opponent, a player must grab them by the arm or round the waist.
5 Every time a player gets back to their team with the ball, they get a point. If a player is 'caught' while running with the ball, the opposing team gets a point. The ball is put back into the circle, and another two contestants stand in the circle.
6 The first team to score five points wins.

Comments

Remember that props are not needed in the above version of the activity, which involves mime entirely. However, if you have space either in the classroom or outside in a hall or playground, the students can actually play the games, using English, as a follow-up to the mimed activity.

Another related activity is to ask students to write rules for games they know, or to make up a game and write the rules for it. Wherever possible, it is worth trying to offer your students the opportunity actually to play the games.

Some of the games given as examples in stage 1, or described or invented by the class, can be based on traditional games from the students' own culture.

6 Sketching a cartoon

Aim: to practise speaking skills.

1 Show the students a cartoon with the caption or speech bubbles covered up, either on the OHP, or as an enlarged photocopy that all the students can see.

2 Do not show the students the caption at this stage. Elicit from the class:
●who they think the characters in the cartoon are;
●where they think they are;
●what their attitudes towards each other might be.
(See example cartoon.)

3 Ask the students to guess what the caption is. Give them a choice that includes the original. For example:

> 1 Perhaps we should take the posters down ...
> 2 Do you think we should open a sweet shop?
> 3 Do you fancy a filling or two?
> 4 Do you play chess?
> 5 _____ ?
> 6 _____ ?

Allow the students to make up their own caption if they wish.
4 Ask the students to write a short dialogue or sketch to include the caption they have chosen. It may come at the beginning, middle or end of their piece.
5 The teacher monitors their progress and helps with ideas and/or language.

6 The students perform their pieces in groups to the rest of the class, who watch and, at the end, identify the caption that was chosen.

Comments

Mixed ability is catered for in stage 3 by allowing the students either to make up their own caption or to choose one from a list provided by the teacher, which may be easier for them. It is also important to allow the choice of either a full-blown sketch or just a dialogue in stage 4.

Where possible, ask students to bring in their own choice of cartoons, which may have captions in their mother tongue. The teacher should translate the caption into English before using the cartoon in class. (Use Tipp-Ex to erase the original caption, and write in an English translation.) Using cartoons brought in by quiet or diffident students should make the activity more accessible to the whole class.

7 Talking pictures

Aim: to practise speaking skills.

1 The teacher or students find a large photograph, or a still from a film showing characters from it. (This can be cut out from a newspaper or magazine. Where possible, use photocopying facilities to enlarge the photograph to a good size.)
2 Elicit information about the context of the picture (who the characters are, where the action takes place, what is happening), and about the film itself, if the students have already seen it or read about it in the local press. If they do not know the film, can they guess the plot and characters from the picture? If, on the other hand, some students are familiar with the film and others are not, let the students in the know say whether the guesses made by the rest of the class are right or wrong. This technique is particularly useful in classes where students have different interests.
3 In groups corresponding in size to the number of people shown in the photograph, students choose a caption and write a dialogue which will include the caption in it.
4 The groups can act the dialogue out, and the class can discuss whether what the groups have written is, as far as they know, what happens (or will happen) in the film.

Comments

It is worth encouraging the students to bring in their own photographs, as this is more motivating for them, as well as easier for the weaker ones.

Groups can be helped by giving them a synopsis of the film (in their mother tongue, if necessary) which will provide a framework for what to write in the dialogue phase.

If you decide to give the groups different photographs from different films, ask the 'audience' to guess which film it is. To make this task easier, you can provide a list of films on the board for the students to choose from.

8 Moving pictures

Aim: to practise writing skills.

1 Give the students a set of pictures that tell a story, as in the example pictures below. These can be photographs from a magazine or textbook, or line drawings from a book of picture compositions, such as D. Byrne's *Progressive Picture Compositions,* or J.B. Heaton's *Composition Through Pictures* (both Longman). The pictures should be given to students in jumbled order.

2 In groups, the students decide on what story the pictures tell, and write it down as a brief scenario.
3 Groups may choose to act out the story they have built from the pictures, with or without words, depending on the time at their disposal and difficulty factors related to the vocabulary, grammar and content of the pictures.
4 As the groups watch each other's versions of the same basic story, they should spot the similarities and differences between them.

Comments

The choice in stage 3 provides the necessary flexibility for groups to be able to work at different levels of difficulty. Furthermore, if one group does choose to mime rather than act out a dialogue, the students should be asked to write a dialogue to go with the mime either in class or as homework. Students who feel in need of support will have both the pictures and the dialogues performed by other groups to help them with the task.

9 *Decontexualised dialogues*

Aim: to practise speaking skills.

1 Take an extract of half a dozen lines from a play, making sure that the language is simple. For example:

> *Bates:* Come with me tonight.
> *Ellen:* Where?
> *Bates:* Anywhere. For a walk.
>   *Pause*
> *Ellen:* I don't want to walk.
> *Bates:* Why not?
>   *Pause*
> *Ellen:* I want to go somewhere else.

(Harold Pinter, *Silence*)

> *Hound:* Well, what's it all about?
> *Cynthia:* I really have no idea.
> *Hound:* How did it begin?
> *Cynthia:* What?
> *Hound:* The . . . thing.
> *Cynthia:* What thing?

(Tom Stoppard, *The Real Inspector Hound*)

> *A:* No.
> *B:* Graham's all right, is he?
> *A:* Yes, he's all right.
> *B:* There's nothing wrong is there?
> *C:* Why don't you mind your own bloody business?

(John Osborne, *The Entertainer*)

(You may supply the class with the names of the characters, as in the first two examples, or replace the names of the characters with letters, as shown in the third. Don't tell the students where the extracts are from until the end of the lesson.)

2   In groups, the students should try and work out the context of the extract you have given them.

> *Who are the speakers?* _____
> *Where are they?* _____
> *How do they feel towards each other?* _____
> *What are they talking about?* _____
> *Are they standing or sitting?* _____
> *What happened just before this extract?* _____
> *What is going to happen next?* _____

(You may work with either one or a variety of extracts, but do make sure that at least two groups have the same extract, for purposes of comparison later.)

3   The groups write a dialogue to include what is said before and after the extract, as well as including the extract itself. The passages supplied by the students may be as long or short as they wish – without being *too* long! (See next stage.)
4   The groups choose students to play the parts in the dialogue (usually two or three at most) and these actors learn the lines by heart. The other members of the group prompt and rehearse them.
5   The groups present their different interpretations of the dialogues. The audience watch and try to guess the context of them using the framework suggested in stage 2 above.

Comments
The flexibility in this exercise lies, on a language level, in the students' freedom to add as little or as much as they like to the extracts. On the level of personality, it allows the students to respond to the dialogue and interpret it as they wish (hence the importance of not giving away too much about the original characters, even in terms of their names.) If further guidance is needed, you can suggest names for the characters or examples of roles they may choose to draw on. For example:

husband/wife	boy/girlfriend	stranger/stranger
friend/friend	employer/employee	teacher/student
enemy/enemy	parent/child	etc.

This exercise works at any level of linguistic sophistication – even at an elementary level – and there is some feeling of satisfaction at the end of the exercise when students are told that they have been working with 'difficult' writers such as Pinter, Stoppard and Osborne.

I would like to end this chapter with a few guidelines for overcoming resistance to what students might consider unorthodox techniques for learning English.

1 Begin with simple activities.
2 Keep the activities brief in the early stages.
3 Build drama activities on textbook work.
4 Do not force students if they are not ready for drama activities: their interest and openness is vital.
5 Allow students to remain silent if they wish to, while others are taking a more active part.
6 Provide enough guidance to allow *all* your students to achieve at least part of the task.
7 Stop the activity if it is not enjoyable.
8 Encourage co-operation; avoid competition.
9 Draw on the students' own experience wherever possible, for ideas and material.
10 Draw on the students' ability to think, their capacity for feeling, and their potential for *doing* rather than just watching.

Further reading

Dougill, J. (1987) *Drama Activities for Language Learning* (Macmillan)

Holden, S. (1981) *Drama in Language Teaching* (Longman)

Maley, A. and A. Duff (1982) *Drama Techniques in Language Learning* (Cambridge University Press)

Spaventa, L. (ed.) (1980) *Towards the Creative Teaching of English* (Heinemann)

Wessels, C. (1987) *Drama* (Oxford University Press)

CHAPTER 9 | The pleasure principle 1

Many of the factors discussed in previous chapters contribute to the success or failure of a lesson. Content alone may not do the trick, but a combination, say, of interesting topics and good teacher-student rapport will create that sense of purposeful, pleasurable activity we learn to recognise, but often find hard to define. Above all, the whole process of learning is helped along if the students derive genuine pleasure from the lesson. This may seem obvious, but it is rarely acted on. Of all classes, mixed ability classes are particularly riddled with differences, of talent, personality and opinion. Yet one thing that all learners, from a wide range of cultures, fortunately seem to agree on is the importance of pleasure. This may take many forms: jokes and humour, performance and entertainment, games, puzzles and mysteries, or just a vague sense of well-being. For the teacher of mixed ability classes, the pleasure principle provides a vast reservoir of ideas which we cannot afford to ignore. It may seem difficult to be an 'entertaining' teacher, but there are principles which should make the task easier.

In this chapter, the importance of the pleasure principle with mixed ability groups is illustrated through the use of particular types of ludic activity: games, quizzes and stories. In chapter 10, I will look at jokes and puzzles. One hopes that most of what one does in the classroom will give students a certain pleasure, but what I am specifically concerned with here are activities which would normally be considered light or even frivolous, and yet which seem to hold a universal attraction.

Games

What is a game? One working definition is that of an enjoyable activity involving an objective that is achieved by following certain rules, usually in competition with one or more other people.

The use of games in language learning has long been accepted and there is now a wide variety of handbooks available to teachers containing games to suit all tastes (see the reading lists at the end of this and the next chapter). However, I do not intend simply to list more games of the type found in these useful books. I will limit myself to those which contribute in a specific way to solving problems that relate to the mixed ability class. *Card* and *board* games are one such source of useful material.

Apart from the pleasurable associations that card and board games have for most people, they provide something essential for large mixed ability classes: flexibility and physical activity. Material in a textbook can be difficult to work with, as the whole class is presented with the same information simultaneously, and there often seems to be no alternative but to go through the exercises in the order given. Neither this order nor the techniques used may be exactly what suits the needs of that particular class. Transferring words from the page onto cards or the board increases the options available to the teacher, especially as regards who gets what information and what can then be done with it.

1 Synonym snap

Aim: to practise the vocabulary encompassed by synonyms and similar words.

1 Write twenty-five or more pairs of equivalent words onto cards, limiting yourself to those covered by previous lessons, which fit into certain grammatical groups (nouns, verbs, adjectives and adverbs, for example). Here are some examples for an elementary level:

Verbs: *speak, talk, look, watch, tell, say, live, stay, start, begin, hate, dislike,* etc.
Nouns: *job, work, skirt, dress, sweater, pullover, boy, girl, sofa, settee, shoes, boots,* etc.

2 Put the pile of cards on a table at the front of the class and split the class into two teams.
3 One player from each team goes up to the table, and the two players take it in turns to turn a card over and read out the word written on it.
4 When two words with similar meanings come up, the players have to shout 'snap!' *(one point).*
5 The player who says 'snap' first must also explain the difference between the two words either by giving an example of how they are used or by giving their mother-tongue equivalents *(one point).* For example, the student may have to differentiate between 'skirt' and 'dress', or 'see' and 'watch'. If the player cannot do this, a member of the same player's team can offer an explanation instead *(half a point).*
This offers valuable team support to every individual participant.
6 When the cards have all been used once, shuffle the pack and start again.

Comments

To speed the game up, have the members of each team standing ready to run to the table. In a large class where, for whatever reason, the teacher does not wish students to get up from their desks, any member of the two teams may shout 'snap' from where they are sitting, as the teacher calls out the words.

2 Family relay

Aim: to practise vocabulary through semantic sets.

1 On cards, write words forming distinct groups. For example:
   Furniture: *chair, stool, settee, table, desk, cupboard, wardrobe, armchair.*
   Animals: *cat, dog, snake, giraffe, mouse, elephant, bird, rabbit.*
   Transport: *car, van, bus, plane, ship, bicycle, train, lorry, motorbike.*
   Clothing: *hat, coat, jacket, shirt, skirt, dress, blouse, tie, cap.*
   Ailments: *cold, headache, toothache, temperature, sore throat, backache.*
2 Shuffle the cards and put them on the table at the front of the class (away from the front of the blackboard).
3 Divide the board into five sections, relating to lexical groups:

FURNITURE	ANIMALS	TRANSPORT	CLOTHING	AILMENTS

4 Divide the class into two teams. Assign each team a different coloured chalk or board-pen. (Make sure the two colours will be clearly visible and distinct.)
5 Explain that a member of each team has to come to the front, take a card, look at the word and decide which group it belongs to. He or she then has to write the word on the board, under the correct category, in the team's colour chalk.
6 The chalk is then passed to the next player who takes another card and repeats the process, as quickly as possible.
7 When all the cards have been used up, the teacher counts up the number of correct words for each team, and declares the winner.

Comments
Although there is a competitive element in this game, the students are not competing as individuals, but as members of a team. There is also an element of luck involved, as in multiple choice activities.

3 Progressive fade-out

Aim: to revise a range of structures.

1 Imagine the aims of the lesson have been 'likes and dislikes'. The board might look something like this:

QUESTION	POSITIVE	NEGATIVE
Do you like ice-cream? Do you like football? What about swimming?	Yes, I do. Yes, I think it's wonderful. Yes, she does. Yes, they do.	No, I don't. I'm afraid not. No, she doesn't like swimming. No, not really.

2 Ask the students to close their eyes, then rub out one of the items on the board, and ask them to tell you which one it was. Rub out another item, and ask another student to recall which one it was. Continue till the board is blank.
3 Ask students to reconstruct on the blank board all the language you have rubbed out.

Comments
Allow weaker students to recall the first and last items you rub off, as they will probably be the easiest, and give them shorter phrases to recall where possible.

Alternatively, ask the students to make short dialogues in open pairs as controlled practice. Erase an item from the board each time a dialogue is completed. Less confident students can go first, reading from a relatively full board; the most fluent members of the class will be able to reconstruct their dialogue from an almost bare board.

Quizzes

General knowledge quizzes are useful in mixed ability classes because they draw on an area of expertise which may appeal to aspects of the learners' personality other than the purely linguistic (see chapter 1). General knowledge is often seen as more relevant to learners than linguistic knowledge and, when incorporated into the language lesson, should therefore encourage greater participation from the class.

A few points to bear in mind when using quizzes in a mixed ability situation:

●The questions should not be too difficult. Easy questions give the maximum number of students the chance to take part and allow the focus to remain on fast and fluent language production.
●The language in which the questions are couched should not, of course, favour the stronger linguists in the class. Keep the vocabulary and structures simple (as in the examples given below).
●Vary the subject area so as to draw questions from the widest possible range of interests in the class (history, geography, music, literature, sport, etc.)
●Include language questions as part of the quiz (grammar, vocabulary

and, particularly, spelling) to give the activity greater validity in the eyes of more sceptical students.

- Include a number of questions drawn from the students' cultural foreground (such as local history or geography) to maximise their motivation and the answerability of the questions.
- Ask students to write their own questions on pieces of paper or cards, and collect them in. These can be known as 'jokers', and they can be shuffled and drawn on to mark the end and beginning of each round of the game (after every five questions, say). This allows students to contribute actively to the session, regardless of ability, by drawing on areas of knowledge in which they feel confident. If you come across questions containing errors of language, correct them as you read them out, without commenting.
- Have a supply of general knowledge questions in reserve so that you don't dry up. For example:

Elementary quiz

1 Who is the president of the United States?
2 Is the president of the United States a Democrat or Republican?
3 What is 15% of 10?
4 Name one famous Spanish painter.
5 What is the capital of Nigeria?
6 Who wrote *War and Peace*?
7 How many symphonies.did Beethoven write?
8 Who won the Oscar for best actress last year?
9 Which jazz musician was known as Bird?
10 What is sodium chloride?
11 What is the name of the secretary general of the United Nations?
12 How do you spell 'sausage'?

Intermediate quiz

1 Who is Nelson Mandela?
2 Where does Sophia Loren come from?
3 What is Baryshnikov well-known for?
4 Who climbed Everest in 1953?
5 Who was the first person in space?
6 What does H_2O stand for in chemistry?
7 In which country can you see the Colosseum?
8 Which country celebrates its independence on 4th of July?
9 How do you spell 'certificate'?
10 Name the four original members of the Beatles pop group.
11 Which is bigger, the Atlantic or the Pacific Ocean?
12 Which famous artist painted the Sistine chapel in Rome?

Upper intermediate quiz

1 In which country would you be if the currency were 'yen'?
2 Which is the most widely-spoken language in the world?
3 Which American president was assassinated in 1865?
4 Who said, 'Give me a stick long enough and I will move the world'?
5 In which sport are the assistants called 'seconds' and the competitors weighed before the contest begins?
6 Who made the film *The Great Dictator*?
7 Describe the French flag.
8 When did people first start watching television? (Accept the nearest answer.)
9 How do you spell 'exaggeration'?
10 Which twentieth-century Spanish painter is famous for his surrealist paintings?
11 Who directed the film *Extra Terrestrial*?
12 What is the difference between 'efficient' and 'effective'?

1 The number of teams you choose to have will depend on the size of the class. In a small class, the teams could prepare themselves first in groups by studying a hand-out of the list of questions (*figure 1*); they can then turn to face the opposing team like in a TV panel game (*figure 2*). In a large class with fixed desks, the students can remain seated as for a normal lesson, but are split down the middle into two large teams (*figure 3*).

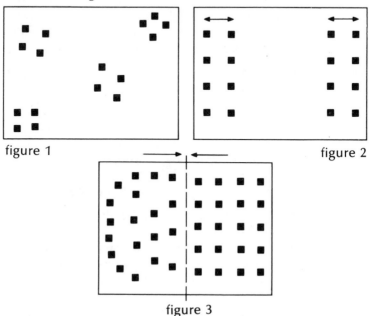

figure 1 figure 2

figure 3

2 Allow the teams to choose team names, such as the names of animals, football teams, colours or makes of car, etc.

3 Start the game by throwing an imaginary ball into the air, which the teams have to 'catch' by answering a question correctly.

4 Allow members of the same team to 'pass the ball' – i.e. delegate a question to another member of the team if they do not know the answer themselves. They should only be allowed to 'pass' once. (Alternatively, teams may be allowed to confer on certain questions but not on others, so as to encourage a spirit of collaboration and support.)

5 A 'foul' may be given for lapsing into the mother tongue, or for whispering or shouting the answer out of turn.

Comments
Students can prepare the questions entirely themselves if they wish, either in groups, for other groups to answer, or as homework.

Stories

The words 'Once upon a time' (and their equivalent in different languages) have a magic which no mixed ability class should be without. Story-telling is something we all do in our everyday lives, and our appetite for cinema, television, theatre and good books indicates the prodigious rate at which we consume stories. Some people are very skilled story-tellers, but for those of us who find people's attention wandering as we approach the punchline of our little anecdote, guidelines do exist for improving our story-telling technique. (See the 'Further Reading' list on page 131.)

One advantage of stories in the mixed ability class is that they provide what Krashen refers to as 'comprehensible input in a low anxiety situation'. There is no obligation for students to speak before they are ready.

'The fact that there is no demand for early speech production reduces the anxiety of the students considerably.'   (Krashen, 1983)

Interesting or amusing anecdotes can be found from the following sources: fairy tales, newspaper reports, short stories (literary), personal experience, films and plays, joke books, textbooks, teachers' handbooks, etc. (See bibliography for specific references.)

The simple adaptation of stories from these sources may make them more interesting and prevent them from falling flat:

- Personalise them by making them refer to your own or the students' experience.
- Choose themes that are of interest to the class as a whole, and adapt stories to make the details refer to familiar situations.
- Build dramatic moments into the story.
- Make the story sound more spontaneous by working from notes, not a complete text.
- Keep eye contact with the class.

For example, in *Once Upon a Time*, Morgan and Rinvolucri re-tell the story of the Pied Piper in a modern Italian setting. When telling this story to Greek students, I highlighted features I knew were familiar to them: the mayor was identified as the then mayor of Salonica; the rats became cars and, of course, caused huge traffic congestion problems; the piper was a bouzouki player (I switched on a tape of the best bouzouki music I could find at appropriate points in the story); the river was the local one, and so on. The following gives an idea of the basic framework of the story:

> There are cars everywhere: in the squares, the streets, on the pavements, up blind alleys, in the parks and churchyards. St Sophia's Square and Aristotle Square both look like car-parks.
>
> Mayor Manavis – alias 'The Greengrocer' – calls the Council together. Outside, people are demonstrating, blaming the traffic on The Greengrocer, threatening to vote for his rival Kouvelas.
>
> Strange bouzouki music is suddenly heard in the distance, faint at first, then getting louder. A stranger appears, who offers to free Salonica of cars, pollution, etc. The Greengrocer offers the stranger a pension, a car and a villa in the country as payment. But the bouzouki player demands one thing: the freedom for children to play in the streets and parks. The Greengrocer agrees. The stranger plays a beautiful tune; at once, engines start up. He leads the cars, buses and lorries to a secret subterranean car-park.
>
> But the mayor does not keep his promise. The stranger plays a different tune and the councillors' cars follow him to River Axios, where they plunge into the water. As his limousine is about to fall in, the mayor promises to build parks and pedestrian precincts –
>
> – The stranger takes off his disguise: he is The Greengrocer's rival, Kouvelas. The people make him mayor instead and he promises faithfully to build an underground metro system and a multi-storey car-park under the sea. And they all live happily ... for a while.

The following techniques are useful for exploiting stories with mixed ability groups.

1 Complete the card

Aim: to provide a reason for listening at different levels of difficulty.

1 Prepare cards with incomplete sentences from the story on them and give one to each student.
2 Ask them to listen to the story and complete their sentences. If necessary, you can give some students more information to work from than others. For example, from the first story above, the following cards may be prepared:

Easier	More difficult
There were too many ...	The people complained ...
There were cars ...	As they were speaking ...
They heard the sound ...	The children had ...

etc.

2 Choose the words

Aim: to encourage students to respond to the story at their own linguistic level.

1 Put a list of words on the board that relate to the story.
2 Ask the students to choose as many words as they wish and, in pairs, to make statements about the story using these words. Some words can be obviously relevant, others less so. For example:

> problem   pollution   anger   promise   claim
> honest   clever   immediately   gradually   deceive
> pedestrian   freedom   unhappy   environment

3 Hold a feedback session with the whole class to share their ideas. These sentences can be recycled later, for use in activities such as that described below.

3 Ranking

Aim: to provide a framework for listening to and discussing the story.

1 Ask the students to rank certain statements in order of their relevance to the story as they see it. Some statements should be simpler than others.
2 Discuss the students' views.

> 1 The mayor was a good man.
> 2 The children were happy.
> 3 The people should not have blamed the mayor.
> 4 The stranger was greedy.
> 5 It was easy to solve the problems of the city.

4 Dicto-comp

Aim: to integrate story-telling with writing.

1 Tell a story in stages. Stop at certain points and ask the students to write down what they think happens next or to describe a particular person or scene.
2 Students should be free to respond at a level that reflects their ability.

3 You might, for instance, ask them to draw parts of the story (as Rinvolucri and Morgan suggest in their book, *Once Upon a Time*). For example, the following might prove fruitful stopping points:

... The people shouted.	*What did they shout?*
... A stranger appeared.	*Describe him.*
... The stranger played a tune.	*What was it like?*
... The stranger asked the mayor to keep his promise.	
	What did he say exactly?
... But the mayor replied.	*What?*
... Then the stranger played a different tune.	
	Finish the story in pairs/groups.

5 Problem-solving

Aim: to practise listening; to invite the students' response to a story by involving them in its plot.

There are points in a story where one can stop and ask students what they would do if they were in that particular situation; for example, (in the story above) if they were the mayor and faced with an angry crowd, or if they were the stranger at the point when the mayor fails to keep his promise. The following is an example of how a story can be approached in this way.

Many years ago, a merchant owed a huge sum of money to a money-lender. The money-lender was old and ugly, and he wanted to marry the merchant's beautiful daughter. He proposed a bargain. He said he would forget the merchant's debt if he could have his daughter instead.

What would you do if you were (a) the merchant (b) the daughter?

Both the merchant and his daughter rejected the proposal. So the cunning money-lender suggested they let luck decide the matter. He told them he would put a black and a white pebble into an empty bag; the girl would then pick out one of the pebbles. If she chose the black pebble, she would become his wife and her father's debt would be cancelled. If she picked out the white pebble, she would be free to stay with her father and the debt would again be cancelled. But if she refused to pick out either pebble, her father would be put in jail.

Would you accept the proposal?

The merchant agreed. The money-lender stooped down to pick up the two pebbles, but the girl saw him picking up two black pebbles, which he put into the bag.

What would you do if you were her?

The money-lender then asked the girl to pick a pebble to decide her fate and that of her father.

> *What should she do?*
>
> The girl pretended to drop her handkerchief. As she picked it up, she also picked up a white pebble, which she then pretended to pick out of the bag.
>
> *How do you think the money-lender responded?*

6 Contradictions

Aim: to practise listening skills and the structure *'should have + past participle'*.

1 Tell the class a nonsense story full of contradictions, and ask them either to write down what is wrong with the story, or (if conditions allow for this noisier version) to call out when they hear anything ridiculous and suggest what the teacher 'should have said'.

> *One fine day . . .*
>
> Yesterday it was rainy, so I took my sunglasses with me. I got into the car and galloped off down the road. When I came to the traffic lights, they were red, so I went straight through them. When they changed, I put the brakes on and drove off. When I got to work, I parked my bicycle and went into the office. There was a lot of work to do, so I sat down and made a few telephone calls. The boss came in and I hit him. Soon, it was time to eat, and I had a lovely big breakfast and drank two glasses of wine. When I got back to the office, my secretary was typing a telephone call . . .

2 One way of encouraging the participation of a broad range of students is to explain to the class that you will only respond to the students' corrections when they use the target structure, 'That's wrong. You should have said . . .'. This repetition of the key language should build the confidence of even diffident students and give them a secure base from which to formulate their answer.
3 As a follow-up activity, ask students to write their own 'contradictions story', but give them the choice of either writing a completely original story or basing it on one from the textbook.

Comments
The original idea for this activity, which may also be useful as a way of revising dull textbook material, comes from the children's rhyme:

> One fine day in the middle of the night,
> Two dead men came out to fight.
> Back to back they faced each other
> Drew their swords and shot each other.   *(Anon)*

Further reading

Lee, W. (1979) *Language Teaching Games and Contests* (Oxford University Press)

Rinvolucri, M. and J. Morgan (1983) *Once Upon a Time* (Cambridge University Press)

Wright, A. (1986) *How to be Entertaining* (Cambridge University Press)

Wright, A., D. Betteridge and M. Buckby (1986) *Games for Language Learning* (Cambridge University Press)

CHAPTER 10 | The pleasure principle 2

Jokes

Jokes are a source of pleasure that the teacher in difficult circumstances will find valuable in a number of ways. They may be used for:

- breaking down barriers and relaxing the class;
- motivating reluctant learners, especially adolescents;
- increasing the students' awareness of cultural factors;
- getting a lesson started, or rounding it off;
- encouraging students to listen and speak for a particular purpose;
- drawing on the students' own experience;
- helping weak learners feel more comfortable by introducing an element of 'play';
- increasing the involvement of the broadest possible range of learners.

The techniques in this section will illustrate these principles, but I will first discuss some preliminary points.

Humour is often culture-specific, whether it is found in the form of cartoons, films or jokes. Some jokes will make some people laugh; others will fall completely, or almost completely, flat. Teachers are often put off by what they consider to be their inability to tell jokes, and it is undeniable that some people have a gift for this, just as some have a natural flair for story-telling. But in teaching we are not aiming at a performance so much as ways of arousing students' interest by varying the material we use and our manner of presenting it. One way round the problem of lack of teacher confidence with jokes is, in fact, to make a joke of this. Some of the ways I have used for exploiting bad jokes include:

- threatening to tell the class a 'bad joke' when they misbehave;
- asking students to listen to, or read, a number of jokes and order them on a scale going from funniest to least funny;
- saying, when a joke falls flat, 'Well, *I* thought it was funny anyway . . .';
- holding a session on what makes different people laugh and why, and on cultural differences in one's sense of humour.

I have found that one does improve with practice. When you have told the same joke to half a dozen different classes, you will find that you say it with more confidence. Above all, I have noticed that good joke-tellers sound as if they are enjoying the telling themselves; they often seem to be keeping themselves from laughing – particularly when they come to the punch-line.

1 Pure and simple

Aim: to use jokes as ice-breakers and lesson-enders for catching the students' attention.

1 Just tell a joke at the beginning or end of a lesson for the sheer fun of it. If you get the ball rolling, your students will often contribute their own jokes. For example:

> *Teacher:* Mario, you should have been here at nine o'clock.
> *Student:* Why, Sir? What happened?

> *Student:* Should somebody be punished for something they haven't done?
> *Teacher:* Of course not.
> *Student:* Good, because I haven't done any homework.

2 Provide the punch-line

Aim: to practise listening and formulating a personal response.

1 Tell the joke, and ask students to supply a punchline. (If necessary, a choice of possible punch-lines can be provided for weaker students.) For example:

There's this old shopkeeper who's very ill in bed. The doctor tells the family that the old man is dying. They rush to his bedroom to say goodbye. The old man is by now nearly blind. He says, 'I'm going to die... Is my wife, Martha, here?'

His wife replies, 'Yes, my darling. I'm here.'

Then the old man says, 'My eldest son, John, are you here?' and the eldest son says, 'Yes, dear father. I'm here.' Then the old man says, 'My second son, Peter, are you here?' And the second son replies, 'Yes, dear father. I'm here.'

[*Repeat the dialogue for his eldest daughter, Elizabeth; his second daughter, Jenny and his youngest son, Benjamin ...*]

At last, the old shopkeeper says, 'So you are all here, are you?' And the family reply, 'Yes, we're all here.'

The punch-line is: 'Then who is looking after the shop?'
Alternative endings: 'Why don't you all go and do something useful?'
'Good. I thought you'd like to know we have no more money left.'
'Did one of you remember to lock the shop up?'

Comments
I learnt this and the CIA joke from Andrew Wilcox.

3 Jokers in the pack

Aim: to use as ice-breakers and for controlled speaking and writing practice.

1 As your students arrive for their lesson, give them each a card with the first or second half of a joke written on it.

2 Ask them to try and memorise their half of the joke and to circulate round the class trying to find their 'other half'. When they have found their partner, they stay together and practise the joke until everyone is in pairs.

3 The pairs then split up and stand at opposite ends of the room to tell their joke.

   Student 1: Waiter! Waiter! What's this fly doing in my soup?
   Student 2: Swimming, I think, sir.
   Student 3: What kind of driver never has accidents?
   Student 4: A screwdriver.   etc.

4 When they have sat down again, collect their cards in and ask them to write down first their own joke and then as many of the other jokes as they can remember.

Comments
A 'seated' version of this activity is also possible. Students say their half of the joke and the student in the class who has the other half responds.

The class gives each joke a score of 0–3 depending on how funny or unfunny they think it is. (This will also ensure that the students who recited their joke first don't stop paying attention.) Weaker students should be allowed to consult their cards if they are having difficulty remembering their extract.

A second possibility is to divide the class into two teams and assign a different coloured chalk or board-pen to each. Shuffle the pack of joke cards and put them on a desk at the front of the class. One member from each team comes to the front, takes a card and copies what it says onto the board. The next member of the team does the same, but whenever a card corresponds to something already copied onto the board, it should be written out next to it to complete the joke. The team with the most completed jokes at the end is the winner.

This activity can also be done by students individually at their desks. The teacher gives out a card to each member of the class and they all copy what their card says into their books. They then return the card to the teacher and ask for another one. As they copy that down too, and the next one, and the next, they try to match as many 'halves' as possible to make as many jokes as they can. The first student to match ten jokes successfully is the winner.

4 Laughter gaps

Aim: to practise listening and speaking.

1 Prepare a worksheet like the following, with the halves of jokes jumbled in two columns.

1 How does an elephant get out of a telephone box?	a Yes, he went mad trying to get rid of his old one.
2 Why was the elephant looking through the window?	b The same way it got in.
3 Jimmy, why don't you share your bicycle with your brother?	c Because it couldn't see through the wall.
4 Did you hear the one about the Australian who bought a new boomerang?	d Because my penfriend can't read very well.
5 Why are you writing that letter so slowly?	e I do. I ride it down the hill, and he rides it up.

2 Ask the students to get into pairs and give a copy of either column 1 or 2 to each student in the pair. Ask them to try and match their information to complete all the jokes.

Comments

When distributing the material, be aware that students may feel securer working with the questions than with the answers, which may prove slightly more demanding of them. The exercise as it stands depends on the availability of photocopying facilities, but where these are lacking, the teacher can read out at random what is in the two columns and the students can shout out 'Snap!' when they hear a complete joke. Keep going until the class have got all the jokes, then ask them to work in pairs to try and write down as many as they can. They can read them out to the class in pairs afterwards.

5 Playing a joke

Aim: to dramatise a joke as a short sketch.

1 Tell the class a longer joke, or write it up on the board.

> There's a Frenchman, an American, an Englishman and an Irishman in a hot-air balloon. They're very high up when the balloon starts to leak and they realise they are beginning to descend very rapidly. They agree that someone must abandon the balloon if the others are to survive and so they decide to draw lots. The lot falls to the Frenchman, who goes to the side of the balloon, says proudly, 'I do this for the glory of France and our marvellous French culture!' and jumps overboard.
>
> The balloon, unfortunately, continues to descend, so once again they draw lots and this time it is the turn of the American. He strolls over to the side of the balloon, looks proudly up at the sky, and as he jumps, says, 'I do this for the glory of America and the free world!' God bless America!'
>
> The Englishman and the Irishman are left alone, but the leak is getting worse, and the balloon continues to descend.
>
> The last lot falls to the Irishman, who, as he is about to jump, says, 'I do this for the greater glory of Ireland!' And he throws the Englishman overboard.

(Notice the reversal of the traditional racist ending to make the joke non-racist.)

2 The students work in groups of four to write a short sketch based on the above joke and act it out for the class. For example:

Frenchman: Mon Dieu! The balloon is descending!
Englishman: How awful!
American: This is is the end of the road!
Irishman: We must do something. etc.

Comments

This joke is a nice one to use, as it can be simplified very easily for students with a low language level. If you want to provide the class with more than one joke or scenario, the performance element at the end may prove more interesting and will thus also cater for a wider scope of talents and taste. The following is another joke that might be suitable in this context:

> A CIA agent goes to a remote mountain village in Scotland. He wants to make contact with a certain secret agent who he knows is there. He goes to the grocer's shop and asks the man behind the counter if he knows someone called McGregor (a common name in that country, like Smith in England).
>
> 'McGregor? There are many men here called McGregor! Which one do you want? McGregor the Meat? He's the butcher. McGregor the Bread? He's the baker. McGregor the Shop? That's me!'
>
> The CIA agent thinks, 'This man is clever. Perhaps *he* is our man.' So he decides to say the code sentence to him, to check.
>
> 'My cadillac has broken down again'.
>
> McGregor the Shop looks at him and says, 'I know! You want McGregor the CIA.'

Both of these jokes work best when adapted to local circumstances; this is easily done by using local, rather than British, place and personal names.

As regards the telling of jokes, it is important that they should not sound as if you are simply reading them out, as this is likely to make them fall completely flat. Even when they are presented as monologues by the teacher, there should be an element of spontaneity in the manner of delivery. This will carry the class along as if it were involved in an informal and friendly conversation, and not a lesson with all its negative connotations.

6 The Socratic joke

Aim: to involve the whole class in telling a joke that is relevant to their local cultural context; to encourage natural speech and spontaneity; to create comprehensible input in an informal classroom atmosphere.

1 Tell a joke using elicitation techniques to create a dialogue with the students. A transcript of the teacher's delivery of the CIA joke in a particular local context might begin something like this:

Teacher:	We read a lot nowadays about CIA agents in Athens. Well, I was reading the other day – I think it was Wednesday – about a CIA agent in Athens who decided to visit a remote mountain village. Why do you think he would want to do that?
Student 1:	To take photographs.
Student 2:	For a holiday.
Student 3:	To contact another secret agent.
Teacher:	Yes, that's right, he went to this village – called Praktohori, I think – to contact the CIA man in the village. There was an important military base nearby, you see. So he arrived there, and where do you think he went to get information? Where in Greece can you get reliable information?

Student 4:   The café.

Teacher: Yes, OK. Now, what do you think the CIA agent is going to say to the man in the café?

Student 5:   Could you tell me where I can find ... whatever his name is.

Teacher: OK. In fact, his name is a very common surname in this country. You know, like in England they have Smith, we have ...?

Students: Papadopoulos!!   etc. etc. ...

Puzzles

In chapter 2, we identified the ability to guess well as one of the characteristics of the successful language learner. This skill forms a part of the problem-solving capacity that is so important to all types of learning. The use of puzzles in the mixed ability class is one way of cultivating this ability to solve problems, because a puzzle is essentially a problem that is presented with the freshness and light-heartedness of a game. A puzzle's ludic quality is an advantage in the mixed ability class as it promotes a positive spirit and a relaxed, 'low anxiety' atmosphere. It allows the focus to centre on process rather than on whether the answer is right or wrong. The kind of puzzles I have in mind include the following:

---

1 A man lives on the tenth floor of a block of flats. Every day he gets into the lift, goes down to the ground floor and leaves the building to go to work. When he comes home, he gets into the lift, stops at the fifth floor and walks the remaining five flights of stairs to the tenth floor. Why?

2 Cleopatra is in bed sleeping; Antony is on the floor next to her bed, dead. How did Antony die?

3 On the lawn of an ordinary English house, there are two small pieces of coal. Why?

4 There is a hut in the desert. It is absolutely empty, except for a dead man hanging by a rope from the ceiling. Outside stands a lorry. What has happened?

5 A girl lies heartbroken on the bed, sobbing. Beside her is a piece of wood. There is a bin in the corner of the room.

6 A man travels to the city by train. On his way home, the train goes into a tunnel. The man immediately throws himself out of the window and is killed.

7 A person passed a window just as a phone rings inside. The person screams.

8 A man is lying dead in the middle of the road. How did he die?

---

1 Interrogating puzzles

Aim: to practise question forms (yes/no and 'wh-' questions).

1 Tell the class one of the above puzzles.
2 Ask the students to get into pairs and prepare at least two questions to elicit more information about the situation described in the puzzle.
3 Guide them by providing a framework such as the following:

A	B
Who ...	Do ...
What ...	Does ...
Where ...	Did ...
When ...	Is ...
How ...	Was ...
Why ...	Were ...
	Has ...
	Had ...
	Have ...

List A gives the class an idea of the kind of information they are trying to find out, in order to be able to arrive at the solution. List B indicates what questions they are allowed to ask.

4 The teacher answers the students' questions until someone guesses the answer to the puzzle. For instance, for Puzzle 1 they might ask:
Does he do this every day?
Does he have a friend on the fifth floor?
Does he like to keep fit?
Is there something wrong with the lift?
Does he work in an office?
Does he have some kind of disability?   etc.

Comments
If it proves too difficult for the students to guess the answer by asking only yes/no questions (column B), some 'wh-' questions (column A), bearing in mind that these are likely to disclose the solution very quickly!

When the students are a bit more familiar with this type of puzzle, they could work in pairs, following the same procedure as described above. Give early finishers another puzzle on separate cards to allow them to carry on working at their own pace.

Task: Here are the answers to the eight puzzles above, in the wrong order. See if you can match them!

The man is a midget.

Antony is a fish.

He had been born blind, but had just had a successful operation to restore his sight. When the train went into the tunnel he thought he had gone blind again.

He was a pilot whose parachute had failed.

The lorry was carrying ice. The lorrydriver was suicidally lonely. He hanged himself by standing on the blocks of ice, which then melted.

The children who lived there had made a snowman and had used the coal for the eyes. The carrot (for the nose) had been eaten by birds.

The man had jumped off a skyscraper believing he was the sole survivor of a nuclear war.

She was the smallest midget in the world. The second smallest midget in the world had sawn off a piece of the stick that she used to measure herself and she thought she had grown taller.

2 Expanding puzzles

Aim: to practise writing skills.

1 After the students have solved the puzzle, ask them to write a brief explanation of it by adding the missing information.

3 Scenarios

Aim: to use puzzles for drama activities.

1 The students get into groups and choose a puzzle to which they still do not know the solution.
2 They devise a situation which they feel will explain the mystery and act this out to the rest of the class, who have to guess which puzzle the group has chosen. If different groups choose the same puzzle to act out, the class can discuss which they think is the best 'solution'.
3 The teacher then reveals the answer to the puzzle, or elicits it from the class, and there is a class discussion about which solution provides the cleverest or most original explanation.

Comments
Give the students the choice of either performing a dialogue or just miming their scenario.

4 Prediction

Aim: to practise oral and writing skills.

1 Give students a few key words from the puzzle before they hear the complete version.

2 Ask them to make a story to include those words. For example:

midget	bin	tears
stick	sawdust	bed

hut	empty	lorry
desert	rope	water

3 Present the puzzle, adding information to help students guess the solution.

5 Hangman

1 Use the 'hangman' idea or 'twenty questions' to set a limit on the number of questions the students can ask.

A puzzle for the reader

> A military aircraft is on an airforce runway. Near it stand the pilot and the engineer. They are talking to the captain. He tells them to fly for three hours in a westerly direction. When they find the target on the map, they are to drop the bomb. The aeroplane takes off. The pilot follows the instructions carefully, and when he is over the target, he presses the button to drop the bomb. Nothing happens. Why?

Further reading

Frank, C. et al (1982) *Challenge to Think* (Oxford University Press)
Granger, C. (1980) *Play Games with English* (Heinemann)
Howard Williams, D. and C. Herd (1986) *Word Games with English* (Heinemann)
King, J. et al (1981) *The Book of British Humour* (Longman)
Spaventa, L. et al (1980) *Towards the Creative Teaching of English* (Heinemann)
Woolard, G. (1991) *Popular Jokes in English* (Macmillan)

CHAPTER 11 | Conclusion

The preceding chapters have examined the problems of mixed ability teaching both on the micro-level of tips and practical strategies, and on the macro-level of pedagogical principle – which should be seen as the binding force behind teaching, making sense of the individual parts and relating them back to the whole. Towards the end of this chapter, you will find the jumbled stages of one (or two) lesson plans, which need to be re-ordered. These are provided as an awareness-raising exercise, and are intended to provoke reflection on the idea of the lesson as an extended and progressive experience.

As stated before, it is difficult to discuss the challenges of teaching mixed level groups without either categorising students unfairly or codifying processes that are by their nature fluid and changeable. Similarly, it is practically impossible to generalise intelligently about the 'ideal' language lesson or, indeed, course. However, it is hoped that through the range of activities presented in this book, and their numerous variations, the reader will gain confidence in the subtle art of adaptation, which can prove so important in the classroom. It is vital to bear in mind that any one activity can be re-conceived a multitude of times, and can thus be gradated to meet a particular mood or need identifiable in the classroom at any one time. This 'choice-potential' has already been discussed, from a specific angle, in chapter 6.

As for the question of adapting the textbook, this is too complex an issue to handle adequately within the constraints of this book. Certainly, there is often a feeling amongst teachers that they are working with inappropriate content, frequently because an author has targeted an age- or socio-economic group that does not reflect their learners' experience and aspirations. Methodology is also often perceived as a problem. It can seem too narrow or unsupportive, providing little or no provision for the early finisher, concentrating too much on particular language skills, or simply assuming a sympathy with a philosophy of teaching that in fact clashes in some way with the teacher's own.

This is not to say that published course materials do not have their value. They certainly provide an abundance of ready-made material, in an order which will satisfy the learners' need for a clear sense of progression; and they remain, at the end of the year, as a concrete record of work done. However, course-books can also be a source of ill-prepared, or mechanical, teaching, and sometimes may appear to support the illusion that pre-fabricated solutions *do* exist for what are actually human problems. Teachers may even feel a book devalues or limits their own skill and inventiveness.

Ultimately, however, the textbook has to be seen as a resource and a 'holding structure', through and within which creative lessons can happen. The following suggestions very much link in with material from chapters preceding this one, but specifically tackle here the issue of the unsatisfactory textbook.

○ One way of making the fixed text on the page more flexible and open-ended is by transferring it to the blackboard in the form of a *grid*. The grid arrangement allows for blocking and grading of the model language in such a way as to permit much greater freedom of movement amongst learners, who can use it at their own level and pace. The teacher can involve the class in building up the grid on the blank board through elicitation techniques, and such personalisation of the material will give the learners a sense of ownership that standard textbooks do not evoke.

○ I have also found that transferring a short passage, or even the language content of a grid, onto *cards* is an excellent way both of getting more static material to 'get up and walk about', and of breaking a text down into smaller, more digestible chunks. Such cards can be distributed amongst the class as a simple and effective means of sharing out language structures, and they will make learners feel actively and positively involved. With them, for instance, students can reconstruct a dialogue, either by each calling out their sentence in sequence while remaining seated, or by memorising what is on their card and leaving it on their desks, to get up and go in search of the fragment preceding or following it.

○ If the original text is recorded on *cassette*, the teacher can play it through and the students put their hands up, either when they hear their extract, or when the teacher pauses the cassette just before their extract is about to come up.

○ Cards can also be used in dictation exercises, either to create a *'collective' dictation*, in which every member of the class has a sentence to read, or to set up a jumbled collective dictation, that becomes a re-ordering activity for students to do in groups or pairs afterwards.

○ Where a course-book stipulates a particularly culture-specific text, students might like to brainstorm all the knowledge they have on the topic before sharing the questions they still need or want answered. Those questions that remain unanswered after the text has been read can then become the basis for research at home or project work.

○ Course-books with storylines can also be a source of dissatisfaction in the classroom, as over-exposure to recurring characters or an insufficiently imaginative plot can turn students off pretty quickly. Again, there is no lack of techniques for softening or postponing this reaction, but those used will depend very much on specific circumstances. Prediction activities, for example, work extremely well with on-going storylines, and if the prediction proves more interesting than the genuine article, there is no reason for not following it through and seeing how far the class can take it. A storyline can also be tampered with by imagining and incorporating a new character – even, if the students like the idea, one of themselves! On a less ambitious scale, students might like to build a comparison between a character or situation in the story and an equivalent from their own experience (leading to role-plays or pair-work dialogues between the new and old characters, if so wished).

○ In the case of broadening the parameters of stipulated tasks, the addition of personalising 'wh-' questions as follow-up to structural or comprehension questions is one good way of keeping early finishers occupied; while incorporating a written element into an oral or group activity can provide a means of monitoring the students' progress unobtrusively, while also encouraging them to use the target language and providing them with a record of work done.

All the above adaptations may be applied as occasionally or intensively as is deemed necessary, and this applies to all textbook adaptations. It is quite possible, for instance, that students will feel more secure using the course-book than they would without it – even if the teacher feels bored. Conversely, the teacher may like the course-book for being solid and 'worthy', but has a class that is fidgeting for more exciting material. Such differences in viewpoint – and they are bound to arise in a large group of people – will have to be aired and resolved as fairly as possible.

(The reader should refer to the index for cross-referencing of activity-types throughout this book.)

Task: Lesson Plan

The stages of the following lesson plan(s) are in the wrong order. Look at the teaching aims below and decide which order you would put them in and why. Are there any other aims you would add to the list? Order the stages of the lesson (A – H) in the sequence you feel most appropriate, then think about what adaptations you might make to the activities to suit them to the kind of students you teach.

Level: Intermediate

Aims:
1 to introduce the Third (or 'Impossible') Conditional;
2 to compare Second ('Unlikely') and Third Conditionals;
3 to use these structures to give advice.

Previous work: Second Conditional

A
Interaction: individual, pair- or group-work, depending on the class.
1 Circulate slips of paper with split sentences on them.
2 The students complete their half-sentences meaningfully. For example, a slip of paper that says: 'If I won the pools...' might be completed: '...I would go the Bahamas.' This may be a written or an oral task.

B

Interaction: pairwork.

1 Give or elicit from the class examples of negative Third Conditionals. For example:
   If I hadn't met you, I wouldn't have got married.
   If I hadn't got married, I would have gone to Australia.
                                                          etc.

2 The students tell each other about a 'problem' they have had, using cue cards.

CARD A	CARD B

YOU...
 	
went to bed late.
didn't hear the alarm.
woke up late.
missed the bus.
got to work late.
were sacked by the boss.
	YOUR PARTNER...
	
	went to a party.
	got drunk.
	walked through a
	   glass door.
	cut him/herself badly.
	went to hospital.
	missed an important
	   interview.

3 They give each other advice, such as: 'If you hadn't gone to bed late, you would have heard the alarm.'

C

Interaction: whole class.

1 Ask the class if anyone has ever met someone famous, such as the Prime Minister or a film star.
2 Ask: 'If you met the Prime Minister, what would you say..?'
3 Ask about other famous people like Gorbachev, Dustin Hoffman, etc., or local celebrities.
4 As the students make suggestions, write their ideas on the board: 'If I met Gorbachev, I would shake his hand.'

Concept Questions: Have you met the Prime Minister?
                                Do you think you will?
                                Have you met Dustin Hoffman?
                                Is it possible you might meet him?

D

Interaction: whole class to pairwork.

1 Put up on the board (or OHP), the following chart.

| If I met | Gorbachev Shakespeare Thatcher | *I would* + verb |
| If I had met | Chaplin Madonna Sophia Loren Garibaldi Andreotti   etc. | *I would have* + verb |

2 The students choose the Second or Third Conditional as appropriate.
3 In pairs, they exchange ideas.
4 Monitor the students as they work.
5 The whole class reports back on what their partner said in their pairs.

E
Interaction: whole class.

1 Write an example of the Third Conditional up on the board: 'If I had met X, I would have asked...'
2 Drill the structure using the names of famous people as prompts (Shakespeare, Cervantes, Alexander the Great, Socrates, John Lennon, etc.).
For example:

> *Teacher:*   If I had met Marilyn Monroe, I would have asked for her autograph. *Shakespeare.*
> *Student:*   If I had met Shakespeare, I would have asked him to write me a poem.
> *Teacher:*   *Cervantes.*
> *Second student:* If I had met Cervantes, I would have asked him about Sancho Panza.
>
>   etc.

F
Interaction: whole-class to individual work.

1 Ask what the students would have asked Charlie Chaplin/Marilyn Monroe/John Lennon if they had met them.
2 Write the students' suggestions up on the board.
3 Ask the students to write two sentences, one Second and one Third Conditional, as in the examples they have provided.

Concept Questions: Have you met Charlie Chaplin?
                             Do you think you will?
                             Is it possible?

G

Interaction: individual, pair and whole-class work.

1   Divide the class into two groups. Group 1 writes the first half of a Second and/or a Third Conditional on a slip of paper; group 2 writes the second half of a Second and/or Third Conditional on a slip of paper.

2   Collect in the slips of paper and put them in two piles at the front of the class in random order. Pairs of students then take it in turns to come to the front and read out the jumbled sentences.
    For example:

> *Student 1:* If I won the pools...
> *Student 2:* ...I would have married her.
> *Student 3:* If I had seen the film...
> *Student 4:* ...I would go on holiday.

3   Ask the class if the sentence is correct and makes sense.

H (pronunciation practice)
Interaction: whole class and individual.

1   Backchain the Third Conditional for rhythm and contractions. Get the students to repeat after you.
    For example:
    • The Great Dictator.
    • about The Great Dictator.
    • asked him about The Great Dictator.
    • I would've asked him about The Great Dictator.
    • Chaplin. I would've asked him about The Great Dictator.
    • If I'd met Chaplin, I would've asked him about The Great Dictator.

Comments

• **Structure**
One of the main problems in presenting the so-called Third Conditional is the sheer length of the structure. It is a major task for students to be able to produce it simply because there is so much of it. This explains the emphasis on controlled practice in the above stages. It is important to help and encourage students to 'get their tongues around the sentence'.

• **Pronunciation**
This most neglected of areas in language teaching is particularly significant when dealing with structures such as the conditionals. If, for instance, the stress does not fall on the words that are most important to the meaning of the sentence, it can be very confusing to the listener.
Notice the way the voice rises on the last important word in the first clause ('If I had met Chaplin') and falls on the last

important word in the sentence ('the Great Dictator'). Notice also how individual words are run together, as if they were one word. For example 'If + I + had + met' becomes 'IfI'dmet'.

● **Meaning**
Concept questions help clarify the differences between 'possible' and 'impossible' conditionals. Although in these lessons the example sentences focus on the distinction between 'dead' and 'alive' (Chaplin as opposed to Gorbachev), in later lessons, other examples of 'impossible' conditionals should be given. (For example, Gorbachev, who may be alive and well, may have visited the students' country a while ago, and in talking about meeting him, it would be appropriate to use the 'impossible' conditional.

● **First, Second and Third Conditionals**
The traditional division is artificial as there are many variations on the conditionals which do not fit these categories neatly. Although it may be pedagogically convenient to begin with such simplifications, students should not be left with the impression that the examples given are the only possible combinations of tenses.

● **The Sequence of Stages**
This will depend on:
1 how far you stick to a 'presentation – practice – production' format;
2 how far one stage depends on the previous one (often referred to as the 'task dependency' principle). For example, the writing task in stage A above clearly depends on the game described in stage G.
3 whether you wish to adopt a 'deep-end' approach, beginning with, say, a communicative activity before going on to a more controlled phase.

The implicit principle behind this whole book has been to highlight how one can avoid setting one's students up to fail, in order to empower them to succeed. Generally speaking, the more students are listened to and valued – both as language learners and as people – the more they will be encouraged to have confidence in themselves. A positive self-image will release them to some degree from any feelings they have of frustration, and even fatalism, and may thus liberate them to tackle their language problems in an energetic and realistic way. If the teacher can be sensitive, flexible and supportive towards all the individuals that make up his or her mixed level class, they will be all the more encouraged to be sensitive, flexible and supportive towards each other – and the teacher – also. Such an atmosphere will unify even the most disparate group of people working together, and help lay to rest, once and for all, the myth of the 'bad' language learner.

A mixed ability glossary

Accuracy   In audio-lingual methodology, error is to be avoided at all costs. Thorough drilling encourages the production of correct sentences. The prioritisation of accuracy generally leads to teacher-dominated lessons and a neglect of communicative or 'fluency' activities.

Acquisition versus learning   'Acquisition' has traditionally been used to refer to the mother tongue and 'learning' to the second or foreign language. The distinction suggests that, while acquisition occurs naturally and unconsciously, learning is a conscious process. Krashen uses the terms in a related sense in his monitor theory, where acquisition is understood to mean picking up a language spontaneously, and learning tends to be what happens in classrooms, particularly when the emphasis is the correct application of rules.

Affective   Referring to the emotions. Humanistic approaches are often described as 'cognitive' or 'affective'.

Audio-lingual   A method which held sway in the fifties and sixties. Based on the principle that learning is largely a process of habit-formation, it stresses the importance of controlled oral practice, mainly in the form of drills and substitution tables. The theory of language underlying this approach emphasises the differences between languages. Thus, the mother tongue is seen as a source of interference, which can hinder the acquisition of a new language. Contrastive analysis would perform the role of identifying these differences, and selecting and grading structures accordingly. The order of presentation of the four skills is usually that of listening, speaking, reading and writing. Structures are embedded in short dialogues, which are often learnt automatically. Meaning is second in importance to structural patterns.

Although communicative methodology has largely replaced audio-lingual methodology as the predominant orthodoxy in ELT, it would seem common-sense in a mixed ability class, often with as many as forty-five pupils in the room, to include aspects of audio-lingualism in one's teaching. The occasional drill or substitution table might be an economical way of building confidence, especially where the accurate manipulation of structures is concerned. Nevertheless, as many of the activities in this book attempt to show, controlled practice need not be mechanical, as in traditional audio-lingual practice. Indeed, the lock-step approach associated with audio-lingual methodology, whereby all the students are locked into the same rhythm under the dominant orchestration of the conductor/teacher at the front of the class, suggests the essential unsuitability of this approach in mixed ability situations.

Authentic An epithet used to refer to material intended for the use of native-speakers – newspapers, maps and railway timetables, for example. There is also a second kind of authentic material, used in EFL contexts and international settings, and that is when non-native speakers use English either within their own community or as a means of communication with other non-native speakers. These applications encompass local varieties of English and English as an international language. This type of authentic usage is important in cross-cultural approaches to language learning, and it is an aspect of mixed ability teaching that is highlighted in this book.

Backchaining This is a technique used in drilling pronunciation, and consists of building up an utterance backwards.

Teacher: cinema?
Pupil: cinema?
Teacher: to the cinema?
Pupil: to the cinema?
Teacher: go to the cinema?
Pupil: go to the cinema?   etc.

The aim is to help the learner produce and maintain the correct stress, rhythm and introduction of an utterance.

Behaviourist A theory of learning based on stimulus-response reinforcement, which became associated with audio-lingual methodology. Behaviourists see little difference between learning a language and learning anything else. According to them, there is no complex internal process going on, there is only what is objectively observable: a stimulus (for example, a command that someone do something); a response (the performance of the action); and reinforcement (a reward of some kind). The influence of behavioural psychology can be seen in the drills popular in audio-lingual approaches.

There may still be a place for this approach to learning wherever the task is basically mechanical – for example, in learning the sounds of the language. It is not adequate, on the whole, as a response to the varied and unpredictable problems of the large mixed ability class.

Cloze A text from which words have been deleted and replaced by blanks. The students may be expected to complete the blanks with the original words or with synonyms. In pure forms of cloze, based on gestalt psychology, the words are omitted on a regular basis (every fifth or seventh word). As the theory of gestalt emphasises the mind's tendency to perceive significant patterns and to complete what is incomplete, its principles provide learners with an opportunity to be 'partly right', and encourage them to trust their previous experience.

As a test, cloze is global (holistic) rather than discrete (or atomistic) (compare it with multiple-choice tests, for example). It is based on a continuous text and therefore requires the use of a variety of skills, both receptive and productive. If we adopt a selective approach to deleting words from a text (see chapters 1 and 6), it will be seen that cloze exercises are flexible and highly suited to mixed ability groups, where the same text may be used at different levels of difficulty.

Cognate   This describes a word that looks similar to one in another language, which may also have a related but not identical meaning. 'False cognates' (or 'false friends') look similar but have different meanings. Both types of cognate provide useful ways of using the mother tongue in the classroom (see chapter 5).

Cognitive   Refers to theories of learning which stress the mind's capacity to understand and organise experience meaningfully. Gestalt theories and the work of Chomsky are cognitive in orientation. The term contrasts with 'behaviourist', which rejects the existence of innate cognitive structures in favour of that of habits formed by a procedure of stimulus – response – reinforcement.

Competence   In the work of Chomsky, this is the speaker's total knowledge of a language system. This knowledge is, for most people, implicit; it is what makes **performance** possible, i.e. the actual occurrence of language in use. Thus, grammar is, in effect, a description of competence, while performance refers to the language produced by particular speakers. While competence is an idealised, perfect form of the language, performance may include errors, slips of the tongue and so on.

'Communicative competence' was coined in response to Chomsky's linguistic competence, and highlights the social context of language use. If accuracy is a part of linguistic competence, appropriacy is an aspect of communicative competence, which is thus concerned with performance rather than an ideal knowledge of a language.

These terms should be compared with **learning** and **acquisition**. They should all help the teacher to decide on objectives, and to assess the relative roles of accurate grammatical knowledge and fluent communication within a clear framework.

Community language learning   A method developed by C. Curran, and based on both counselling psychology and the social dynamics of the group. It is student-centred and draws on the group's supportive capacities. The students suggest the topics for discussion, and the teacher's role is to help sustain the activities without forcing any student to participate who does not want to. A collaborative effort is encouraged, and reflective sessions are held to think about the learning process, and discuss the class's goals and expectations. The learners sit in a circle, facing each other, and decide what they want to speak about – in their first language initially if they want to, and later in the foreign language. The teacher, sitting outside the circle, provides target language equivalents, which the learner repeats. Like other humanistic approaches, this method attempts to reduce the learners' anxiety by encouraging them to develop their own inner criteria for evaluating what is learnt and activating their emotional resources.

Comprehensible input From Krashen's input hypothesis, referring to messages the students can understand. They need plenty of comprehensible input, presented in low-anxiety situations, in order to acquire a language naturally.

Contrastive analysis A comparison between two languages, especially between the learners' mother tongue and the target language. The basic assumptions behind traditional contrastive analysis (associated with audio-lingual approaches to language learning) are that (a) structures which are similar in the two languages are easy to learn and, conversely, elements which are different are difficult to learn; and (b) the majority of errors made are the result of mother-tongue interference. Both assumptions have been questioned, and the latter now rejected by Krashen in his monitor theory. This has obvious implications for the use of the mother tongue in the classroom.

Context The fact of being written or spoken; the relationship between speakers or writers; the formality or informality of a message; the attitudes of the speaker or writer, and so on.

All utterances occur in a context. The context of communication creates the conditions for appropriacy of language use, and thus complements the concept of accuracy, which tends to be associated with specific items seen in isolation. The concept of 'defective but effective' communication, and the consequent tolerance of non-significant error, may help learners to establish the confidence to loosen their tongues!

Correctness This concept goes back to grammar/translation approaches with their strong, prescriptive emphasis; for example, assertions such as 'It is wrong to end a sentence with a preposition', or 'The *real* meaning of "aggravate" is to "make heavier" ' are typical. Since the rise of descriptive linguistics in the twentieth century, however, the trend has been to describe what people *actually* say, not what they *should* say. The notion of correctness is now to be related to that of appropriacy; thus a knowledge of language use is considered to be as important as a knowledge of the rules of the grammar. If this means more recognition of the value of small group-work in practising communication, then the emphasis on appropriacy rather than accuracy should make mixed ability teaching easier.

Deductive A deductive approach to learning gives rules first, before going on to provide concrete examples and practice of the rule. Grammar/translation approaches are generally deductive.

Deep-end Traditionally, a lesson is approached in three stages: presentation – practice – production. Thus, the new material is presented by the teacher and practised in drill-like activities, before an opportunity is given for 'free' practice of some kind. The 'deep-end' technique begins with a 'free' or communicative activity, allowing students to use any language they have at their disposal; on the basis of how students manage in this phase, the teacher diagnoses what language needs to be presented for the successful fulfilment of the task.

The advantages of 'deep-ending' in a mixed ability class are that (a) good students are given an opportunity to perform at a level appropriate to their ability, while the teacher monitors the weaker learners; (b) a need is created in the learners for the language practice that follows, and this helps motivation; (c) students are involved in what is often a short lesson, from the very beginning; (d) the teacher does not waste time presenting material that is either too easy or too difficult for the class.

Dictation   The conventional dictation procedure, going back to grammar/translation, involves reading a text three times at a slow pace, with pauses on the second reading to allow students to write the text down. Traditionally, the texts used are short narrative extracts.

Dictation began to regain some of the popularity it had lost in the seventies when research recently found it to be a more reliable testing device than, say, multiple choice. It is also gaining popularity as a teaching device, thanks largely to the publication of *Dictation* by Davies and Rinvolucri. Dictation is, in fact, a flexible and highly expressive form of language use, and it requires little preparation.

Direct method   This method, dating from the late nineteenth century, was characterised by the avoidance of the mother tongue and an emphasis on the spoken language – in contrast to the grammar/translation approach, to which it was a reaction. It is based on how children learn their mother tongue, and uses context (pointing to objects, performing actions) to make meaning clear. As phonetics became prominent at around that time, this was reflected in the direct method's emphasis on pronunciation. It has been enormously influential as a methodology, and a more rigorous version – that of Total Physical Response (based on humanistic principles, and associated with monitor theory) – has become popular, especially in the USA.

Discrete item/point   This refers to tests where one item of language is tested at a time, as in multiple choice or grammar tests. These tests may be easier to mark, but they do not test a range of items or skills in the integrated manner that cloze or dictation tests do. Cloze and dictation can for this reason be made more responsive to the diverse needs of the mixed ability class.

Drama techniques   These include sketches, mime and plays (theatrical activity in the traditional sense) but do not necessarily lead to a performance. Drama in TEFL also includes improvisation, role-play, simulation and a wide variety of game-like activities involving the emotions, physical activity and the exercise of the imagination. Drama activity sensitises the learner to voice, movement, facial expression and gesture, and its open-endedness makes it a valuable (if difficult) approach to adopt in the mixed ability class, rewarding to both learners and teacher in the long-run.

Error   As opposed to 'slips' or 'mistakes', errors occur regularly or systematically. They typify an individual's or a group's learning strategies and are therefore an important – and positive – aspect of learning a foreign language. They should not be allowed to become a source of anxiety for 'weak' learners.

Four skills   These are the skills of listening, speaking, reading and writing. Traditionally, reading and listening have been referred to as 'passive' skills, but it is more common now to refer to them as either receptive or even active processes, just as we do speaking and writing (traditionally, the 'productive' skills). Whereas reading and writing are given priority in grammar/translation approaches, in audio-lingual approaches, the reverse is true. Communicative methodology, on the other hand, gives equal weight to these skills and their sub-skills, and also emphasises the importance of integrating them through such techniques as information-transfer.

Global   (a) In 'global' listening, a text is listened to in its entirety in order to give students an overall understanding of it, thus practising a sub-skill of listening.

(b) 'Global proficiency' refers to the students' ability to apply a variety of language skills in order to understand or produce a text. For example, a composition, cloze test or dictation all test global proficiency.

(c) A 'globally' designed textbook is one intended for use all over the world in a variety of countries, rather than one locally produced for a particular market.

(d) 'Global' culture emphasises the need for different nations and organisations to co-operate to solve international problems (such as those related to the environment).

Grammar/translation   A method of teaching foreign languages that was originally applied to the teaching of Latin and Greek. The main teaching aids are the grammar book, dictionary and reader. The procedure for learning would involve: translating a text from the reader orally; conjugating verbs; declining nouns; learning rules and exceptions to rules; doing dictations; the use of literary texts generally. The foreign language is hardly used in class except in order to complete text-based comprehension questions. Oral communication is minimal, and the main focus is on translating written texts. Although this method is still practised sporadically, its only value to the mixed ability class is its acceptance of the role of the mother tongue, which has a certain part to play in helping weaker learners participate in the lesson.

Group- and pair-work   In traditional frontal or lock-step approaches, the teacher dominates the presentation – practice – production sequence of a typical lesson. Group- and pair-work not only reduce teacher-talking time, converting the teacher's role into that of co-ordinator, facilitator and advisor, but also allow 'weaker' learners both to take a more active part in class and to work at their own pace. The shy student can also avoid the embarrassing glare of public performance. In short, group- and pair-work are essential in mixed ability situations.

The need to encourage a natural use of language has also made group- and pair-work indispensable, as talking *at* someone is very different from talking *to* them.

However, badly-planned group- and pair-work can backfire, just as can overuse of the mother tongue. It is therefore important (a) for pupils to know why the task they are doing has been set as a group-work activity; (b) for the teacher to demonstrate what is required with models, examples and explanations; (c) to ensure that there is either an information or opinion gap to make communication exchange necessary and fruitful; (d) to supply appropriate material for the realisation of the task; (e) to set a time-limit; (f) to arrange the desks appropriately; (g) to appoint group-leaders or secretaries where appropriate.

Individualisation   The teaching technique whereby the learner's independence is encouraged, the teacher's role being to provide material and tasks according to students' individual needs. This contrasts with how traditionally the teacher (or school) imposes a syllabus and methodology. Individualisation programmes are learner-centred and aim to encourage autonomy through self-directed learning strategies. An important element in individualisation is *choice*: it is the student who decides what to learn and how, and the student learns at his or her own pace. The theory is that by being made aware of the learning process, the learner may thus adopt more efficient learning strategies (see chapter 2). Material organised on a 'self-access' basis, and many of the programmes designed for the micro-computer, are in keeping with individualisation.

Inductive   Giving examples and practice before stating rules explicitly. Audio-lingual approaches are inductive.

Information gap   A feature of communicative methodology. The basic idea is that some students possess information that others do not; the latter are thus obliged to use the language they know to acquire this information – to fill the gap. Thus, the information gap is a device for encouraging a purposeful use of language in the classroom. Very useful in a mixed ability class, in that the stronger students may be given the task of asking questions to acquire information held by their partner, whose contribution would thus be easier – if no less important to the success of the activity.

Information transfer   These techniques involve the learner in inter-preting a written or spoken text and then transforming the relevant parts of it into a non-verbal form: a table, chart, diagram, flow-chart, application form, etc. The use of such exercises marks a shift away from the exclusive use of comprehension questions of the yes/no or 'wh-' question variety, and thus reflects a greater interest in the learner's ability to focus on important information and ignore what is irrelevant. The learner also has the opportunity to practise a variety of sub-skills, such as listening for gist, note-taking, summarising, prediction, etc. It is assumed that the ability to state information in a non-linguistic form – for example, by completing a diagram – reflects the learner's understanding of a text as effectively as answering conventional comprehension questions. In a mixed ability class, information transfer has several advantages (see chapter 7).

Integrative   Involving more than one aspect of language or more than one language skill. Integrative motivation is when the learner wishes to learn a foreign language in order to become an active member of the foreign language community. (See also **motivation**, below.)

Interlanguage   An interlanguage – the stage a learner's competence in a foreign language has reached at any particular moment – marks the learner's continuing attempt to achieve mastery of a language, and is characterised by recurring errors. However, as these errors indicate a stage in the learner's development, they should not be seen as a sign of weakness, but as a measure of progress. The attempt to eradicate errors at all costs may demoralise the learner unnecessarily, and can exacerbate the problems encountered with a mixed ability class.

Learning   (See **acquisition**, page 149.)

Listening   An active process, requiring not only the recognition of sounds and their meanings in isolation, but also the understanding of contextual features such as the relationship of the speakers, the speakers' setting, their implicit attitudes, and so on. Listening can be extensive (global) or intensive (focusing on detail). Global listening encourages students to listen for gist (an important sub-skill), and thus material may be used that is above the level of particular students. In a mixed ability class, the concept of listening as an activity made up of a variety of sub-skills (prediction, listening for gist, guessing and inferring meaning, etc.) will help the teacher to involve more learners at a variety of levels of difficulty. The text may remain the same, but the tasks are graded.

Listening is preferably practised in relation to other skills or even to non-linguistic tasks, such as completing a diagram or filling in a chart. The importance of listening for language students who are experiencing difficulties is highlighted by the place it has in Krashen's comprehensible input theory and in methods such as Total Physical Response. In both cases, the learner is allowed to listen in the early phases of learning without having to speak, building up a knowledge of the language through abundant, passive exposure to messages that are made clear by the context in which they are uttered.

Lock-step   This is when the teacher conducts the lesson from the front of the class, obliging all students to proceed at the same pace in spite of any differences in their learning styles or level. This may be motivated by a desire to correct errors as soon as they occur. Such an approach is likely, however, to raise anxiety levels in the mixed ability class.

Micro-computer   Potentially a great help to the mixed ability teacher, in that programmes designed as tests or teaching devices have the flexibility to allow learners to work at their own pace, often with material of their own choice. The feedback a student gets – correction, praise, or further information – is impersonal and unembarrassing.

Motivation   This may be *intrinsic* or *extrinsic*. It is intrinsic when the learner finds the subject interesting in itself or useful in fulfilling personal aims. Motivation that is imposed from the outside in the form of tests, rewards or threats of punishment is extrinsic. *Instrumental* motivation refers to language learning that is done for a limited purpose as a means to an end, such as for a holiday abroad, or in order to pass an examination. *Integrative* motivation is in operation when the language learner wishes to become a member of the community in which the language is spoken. This involves the learner's identification with native speakers of the language and their culture. The problems of the mixed ability class are often exacerbated by the students' lack of intrinsic motivation or by their resistance to the teacher's – misguided – attempts to 'sell' them the culture of the target language.

Natural approach   Originally used at the turn of the century as a synonym for the Direct Method, but now associated with techniques developed from Krashen's theory of comprehensible input.

Performance   In Chomsky's theories, this is what is actually said or written in a language, as opposed to the idealised knowledge of the language, referred to as 'competence'. (See **competence**.)

Questions   Grammatically, of three basic types:

●yes/no (polar) questions;
●either/or questions;
●'wh-' questions (*what, how, why,* etc.).

These question types may be ordered according to difficulty. For example, yes/no questions are often relatively easy because part of the answer is contained in the question itself; 'who' and 'where' questions tend to be easier than 'why' and 'how' questions because they are usually more factual and less conjectural.

In dealing with a text, the teacher may wish to grade the questions on the basis of content. For example: (a) questions for which there is a word-for-word answer in the text; (b) questions for which an implied answer may be found in the text; (c) questions which demand a personal response from the learner, based on their *interpretation* of the text. The full potential of questions in the mixed ability class is explored in Morgan and Rinvolucri's *The Q Book*.

Reading   An active, not a passive, process made up of a wide range of sub-skills, including prediction, guessing or inferring from context, reading for gist, skimming a text quickly, and scanning for specific information. The pendulum has swung both for and against reading in the history of ELT, from its predominance in the grammar/translation approach, to its relative neglect in audio-lingual approaches. In communicative methodology, it has received more attention as the emphasis on learner needs has led teachers to recognise that reading is an important skill for a large number of learners, who will need to read rather than speak the language. In the mixed ability class, reading has an important part to play in providing anxiety-free activity for shy and weak learners, as they are not required to produce language in front of the rest of the class. It is also a skill that they can develop in their own time with the use of simplified readers.

Self-access   A way of extending normal classroom activity by enabling students to work on their own. Material is made available to the students and they can select from it according to their personal needs. The material may be in the form of reading texts, grammar exercises, or listening texts on cassette, with self-explanatory instructions and model answers where appropriate. A simple form of self-access is a collection of readers classified according to level; a listening library is similar, but has cassettes instead of books. The flexibility of this approach has obvious advantages for the mixed ability class.

Silent Way   One of the so-called 'humanistic' approaches, developed by Caleb Gattegno. In this method, the learners do most of the talking and are encouraged to build up their own 'inner criteria' for what is appropriate or correct, with a minimum of teacher intervention. The teacher avoids giving the students overt approval in order to encourage self-reliance and the satisfaction of their 'inner criteria'. (Compare this with the emphasis in the audio-lingual method on positive and negative 'reinforcement' from the teacher.) Errors, in the Silent Way, are regarded as an indication of the development of the learners' inner criteria. Structures are introduced via rods of different sizes and colours; the students recall and try to imitate the teacher's presentation. A chart is pointed to (silently) to elicit language from the students. Pictures and readers are also used. Like other humanistic approaches, the Silent Way stresses the role of the individual in learning and tries to activate his or her personal needs and emotions in a relaxed and supportive atmosphere.

Speaking   This skill has received priority since the Direct Method's rejection of the grammar/translation approach at the beginning of the century. Structural linguistics, which influenced the audio-lingual approach, also assert the primacy of speech over writing, and seek to activate oral 'fluency' through highly controlled drills. In communicative approaches, oral skills are integrated with other skills, especially listening, and dialogues aim to practise meaningful language use. Speaking in order to complete a communicative task, whether an information-gap activity or the discussion of a particular topic, encourages classroom interaction and enables the teacher to monitor students during group- and pair-work activities, and to give advice and support to those who particularly need it.

Suggestopedia   This approach to learning, devised by the Bulgarian psychologist, G. Lozanov, is based on the concept of 'waking-state suggestion' – i.e. the attempt to create a pleasant and trusting environment for learning, by tapping both conscious and sub-conscious impulses. Suggestopedia has been developed to activate the reserve capacities of the brain, which it is believed are under-used. Mental and emotional capacities are equally important in learning. Confidence in the teacher's authority is important, but so also is the idea of learning as a relaxed and enjoyable activity. The atmosphere may be influenced and enhanced by the teacher's gestures, facial expressions and tone of voice. Classical music in the background and comfortable furniture help to lower the learner's inhibitions and overcome the fear of error, which is crucial to the mixed ability class.

Testing   Tests may be subjective in nature (composition, for example) or objective (for instance, multiple choice); they can be formal (as with end of year or end of term exams) or informal (such as unofficial assessment during the normal course of teaching). They should always, however, have 'face validity' (*does the test seem relevant in the eyes of the students?*), 'content validity' (*does it test what has been taught?*) and 'construct validity' (*is it consistent with the aims and theory that have influenced your teaching?*). The teacher's approach to tests may either boost the learners' confidence in themselves and their willingness to work together in a supportive way, or it may demoralise them or set them in competition with each other in an obsessive drive for praise and good marks. This distinction is obviously a vital one in mixed ability teaching, where differences in confidence and linguistic aptitude amongst learners may be strikingly large. The failure to separate our constructive teaching/ learning procedures from negative testing ones can often nurture distrust, divisiveness and insecurity in a mixed ability situation.

Total Physical Response   The method developed by Asher whereby learners are given commands and instructions requiring a physical response; for example, 'Stand up,' 'Give your pen to the student sitting next to you,' etc. The method has its origins in the Direct Method and in psychological theories of memory which link learning to physical activity. The method does not make linguistic demands on the learner in the early stages – the learner is not required to speak, but simply to listen, understand and perform the required actions. Stress is reduced through ludic activities and a positive learning atmosphere. Total Physical Response is often associated with humanistic approaches to language learning and to Krashen's theory of comprehensible input.

Bibliography

Abbot, G. (1984) 'Should We Start Digging New Holes?' (*English Language Teaching Journal*, Vol. 38/2)

Adaskou, K. et al (1990) 'Design Decisions on the Cultural Content of a Secondary School Course for Morocco' (*English Language Teaching Journal*, Vol. 44/1)

Alptekin, C. and M. Alptekin (1984) 'The Question of Culture' (*ELT Journal*, Vol. 38/1) For a cross-cultural approach to ELT.

Atkinson, D. (1987) 'The Mother Tongue in the Classroom – A Neglected Resource?' (*ELT Journal*, Vol. 41/4)

Bartram, B. and R. Walton (1991) *Correction* (Language Teaching Publications)

Bertoldi, E., J. Kollar and E. Richard (1988) 'Learning How to Learn English' (*English Language Teaching Journal*, Vol. 42/3)

Bolitho, P. (1983) 'But Where's the Teacher?' (*Practical English Teaching*, Vol. 3/3) For a practical approach to Community Language Learning.

Brown, G. (1990) 'Cultural Values: the Interpretation of Discourse' (*English Language Teaching Journal*, Vol. 44/1)

Brumfit, C. (1980) *Problems and Principles in English Teaching* (Pergamon) For an emphasis on the educational role of the teacher.

Candlin, C. (ed.) (1981) *The Communicative Teaching of English* (Longman)

Carver, D. (1983) 'The Mother Tongue and English Teaching' (*World Language English*, Vol. 2/2)

Cook, V. (1983) 'What Should Language Teaching Be About?' (*ELT Journal*, Vol. 37/3)

Cunningsworth, A. (1984) *Evaluating and Selecting EFL Teaching Materials* (Heinemann) For ideas on adapting textbooks.

Davis, P. and M. Rinvolucri (1988) *Dictation* (Cambridge University Press) For a treasure trove of ideas on open-ended uses of dictation.

Dougill, J. (1987) *Drama Activities for Language Learning* (Macmillan)

Duff, A. (1990) *Translation* (Oxford University Press)

Edge, J. (1990) *Mistakes and Correction* (Longman)

Ellis, G. and B. Sinclair (1990) *Learning to Learn English* (Cambridge University Press)

Fisiak, J. (1981) *Contrastive Linguistics and the Language Teacher* (Pergamon) For useful chapters by Marton on practical uses of the mother tongue in the classroom.

Frank, C., M. Rinvolucri and M. Berer (1982) *Challenge to Think* (Oxford University Press) For ideas on puzzles.

Frank, C. and M. Rinvolucri (1983) *Grammar in Action* (Pergamon) For humanistic and game-like activities.

Freire, P. (1970) *Cultural Action for Freedom* (Penguin) This deals with teaching the mother tongue as a form of consciousness-raising for social change. It shows passion and commitment in education and is essential for teaching in difficult circumstances.

Freire, P. (1972) *Pedagogy of the Oppressed* (Penguin) Essential for a perspective on social commitment in education, and on teaching as a form of ideological, cultural action.

Gattegno, C. (1970) *What We Owe Children* (Routledge) For an analysis of the educational role of the teacher and the importance of sub-ordinating teaching to learning.

Granger, C. (1980) *Play Games with English* (Heinemann)

Grant, N. (1987) *Making the Most of Your Textbook* (Longman) Possibly the fullest treatment of ways of adapting the textbook.

Greenwood, J. (1988) *Class Readers* (Oxford University Press) For a creative, drama-based approach to readers and literature.

Hemingway, P. (1986) 'Teaching a Mixed-Level Class' (*Practical English Teaching*, Vol. 7/1)

Harmer, J. (1983) *The Practice of English Language Teaching* (Longman) For an overall view of theory and practice and especially sections on the role of the teacher.

Holden, S. (1981) *Drama in Language Teaching* (Longman)

Howard-Williams, D. (1986) *Word Games with English* (Heinemann)

Howatt, A.P.R. (1984) *A History of English Language Teaching* (Oxford University Press)

King, J. et al (1981) *The Book of British Humour* (Longman) An essential collection of jokes with which to entertain the mixed ability class.

Krashen, S. (1982) *Principles and Practice in Second Language Acquisition* (Pergamon) A classic exposition of monitor theory and comprehensible input.

Krashen, S. and T. Terrell (1983) *The Natural Approach* (Pergamon) For ideas on what comprehensible input means in terms of classroom practice.

Ladousse, G.P. (1984) *Speaking Personally* (Cambridge University Press)

Lawlor, M. (1988) *Inner Track Learning* (Pilgrims) A handbook, with cassette, on affective, humanistic approaches; important for demonstrating the potential of all learners.

Lee, W. (1979) *Language Teaching Games and Contests* (Oxford University Press)

Maley, A. and A. Duff (1982) *Drama Techniques in Language Learning* (Cambridge University Press)

Morgan, J. and M. Rinvolucri (1984) *Once Upon a Time* (Cambridge University Press)

Morgan, J. and M. Rinvolucri (1988) *The Q Book* (Longman) For ways of personalising interrogatives and giving students something worth talking about.

Nolasco, R. and L. Arthur (1987) *Conversation* (Oxford University Press)

Nolasco, R. and L. Arthur (1988) *Large Classes* (Macmillan) For a practical approach to teaching in difficult circumstances; essential reading for the mixed ability teacher.

Norman, D., V. Levihn and J. Hedenquist (1986) *Communicative Ideas* (Language Teaching Publications)

Norris, J. (1983) *Language Learners and their Errors* (Macmillan)

Nuttall, C. (1982) *Teaching Reading Skills in a Foreign Language* (Heinemann)

Porte, G. (1988) 'Poor Language Learners and Their Strategies for Dealing with New Vocabulary' (*English Language Teaching Journal*, Vol. 42/3)

Prodromou, L. (1983) 'Dictation: Pros, Cons, Procedures' (*Forum*, Vol. XXI/1)

Prodromou, L. (1988) 'English as Cultural Action' (*English Language Teaching Journal*, Vol. 42/2)

Prodromou, L. (1992) 'Cross-Cultural Factors in Language Learning' (*English Language Teaching Journal*, Vol. 46/1)

Revell, J. (1979) *Teaching Techniques for Communicative English* (Macmillan) A classic introduction to practical communicative techniques.

Rinvolucri, M. (1984) *Grammar Games* (Cambridge University Press) For ideas for putting pleasure and personality back into structures.

Rinvolucri, M. (1986) 'Strategies for a Mixed Ability Group' (*Practical English Teaching*, Vol. 7/1)

Rixon, S. (1981) *How to Use Games in Language Teaching* (Macmillan)

Robinson, G.L.N. (1985) *Cross-cultural Understanding* (Pergamon) For research background to chapter 5 of this book.

Rogers, J. (1971) *Adults Learning* (Oxford University Press) For a broad, educational perspective on helping mixed ability adults to learn, also ideas on group-work.

Rubin, J. (1987) 'What the Good Language Learner Can Teach Us' (*TESOL Quarterly*, Vol. 9/1)

Scheibl, R. (1984) 'Tips for Mixed Ability Classes' (*Practical English Teaching*, Vol. 4/4)

Spaventa, L. (ed.) (1980) *Towards the Creative Teaching of English* (Heinemann) For ideas on drama, songs and puzzles.

Stern, H.H. (1983) *Fundamental Concepts of Language Teaching* (Oxford University Press)

Stevick, E. (1986) *Images and Options in the Language Classroom* (Cambridge University Press)

Svarnes, B. (1988) 'Attitudes and Cultural Distance in Second Language Acquisition' (*Applied Linguistics*, Vol. 9/4)

Tomlinson, B. (1987) 'Good Friends' (*Modern English Teacher*, Vol. 15/1) For ways of using words similar in the first and foreign language.

Underwood, M. (1987) *Effective Class Management* (Longman) A practical book on the role of the teacher in the classroom.

Ur, P. (1988) *Grammar Practice Activities* (Cambridge University Press) Fertile, down-to-earth, and full of ideas suitable for the mixed ability classes.

Valdes, J.M. (1986) *Culture Bound* (Cambridge University Press) An approach to teaching the cultural background, rather than foreground, especially in the USA.

Wenden, A. and J. Rubin (eds.) (1987) *Learner Strategies in Language Learning* (Prentice-Hall)

Wessels, C. (1987) *Drama* (Oxford University Press)

Widdowson, H. (1984) 'The Incentive Value of Theory in Teacher Education' (*ELT Journal*, Vol. 38/2)

Willis J. (1981) *Teaching English Through English* (Longman)

Woolard, G. (1991) *Popular Jokes in English* (Macmillan)

Woulfe, P. (1981) 'Exploiting False Friends' (*Modern English Teacher*, Vol. 9/2)

Wright, A., D. Betteridge and M. Buckby (1986) *Games for Language Learning* (Cambridge University Press)

Wright, A. (1986) *How to be Entertaining* (Cambridge University Press) Designed for students, but essential for mixed ability teachers.

Wright, T. (1987) *Roles of Teachers and Learners* (Oxford University Press) For a thorough treatment of the subject, relating theory to practice, with tasks for the reader.

Appendix

The following are the results of a mother-tongue survey, based on work carried out by L. Prodromou in Greece (see *English Language Teaching Journal*, Vol. 46/1, 1992).

58% of all students thought the teacher should *know* the students' mother tongue.
66% (beginners), 58% (intermediate), 29% (advanced) thought the teacher should *sometimes* use the mother tongue.

(Similar figures resulted on the question of whether students should use the mother tongue.)

(In the following statistics, figures in brackets refer to beginners, intermediate, and advanced levels, respectively.)

When the teacher may use the mother tongue:
  Explaining new words (25%, 35%, 18%)
  Explaining grammar (31%, 7%, 0%)
  Explaining differences between English and L1 grammar (27%, 4%, 6%)
  Explaining communicative use of grammar in English and L1 (33%, 22%, 20%)
  Giving instructions (3%, 9%, 0%)

When students may use the mother tongue:
  Discussing pair- and group-work exercises (22%, 2%, 3%)
  Asking 'How do you say X in English?' (13%, 36%, 26%)
  Translating word into L1 to show understanding (18%, 13%, 6%)
  Translating texts into L1 to show understanding (21%, 7%, 6%)

When both the teacher and students may use the mother tongue:
  Checking listening comprehension (27%, 9%, 3%)
  Checking reading comprehension (14%, 7%, 6%)
  Discussing methods (21%, 13%, 6%)

Index